FALLUJAH MEMOIRS

A Grunt's Eye View of the Second Battle of Fallujah

Alexander Saxby

ISBN-13: 9798740492940

Cover photo: 3rd Platoon, Bravo Company, 1st BN 8th Marines, July 2004. All photos are from the authors collection unless otherwise specified.
Printed in the United States of America

I would like to thank my wife, Michelle, for all her love and support. I would also like to thank Chris Wilkins, Daniel Bystricky, Samuel Crist, Robbie Landers, Beth Houck and Micheal Rodriguez for helping with the photographs, and providing invaluable feedback and encouragement.

"Remember the American combat infantryman. The wind, rain and mud boys. The guys no war can be won without"

ERNIE PYLE

In Memory of...

Sergeant Lonny Wells 11-9-2004

Sergeant R.J. Jimenez II 11-10-2004

Corporal Nathan R. Anderson 11-12-2004

Corporal Nicholas L. Ziolkowski 11-14-2004

Lance Corporal Travis R. Desiato 11-15-2004

Lance Corporal Billy L. Miller 11-15-2004

Lance Corporal Bradley L. Parker 11-15-2004

Lance Corporal Dimitrios Gavriel 11-19-2004

Corporal Gentian Marku 11-25-2004

Lance Corporal Jeffery S. Holmes 11-25-2004

Lance Corporal David B. Houck 11-26-2004

Corporal Kirk J. Bosselmann 11-27-2004

Lance Corporal Joshua E. Lucero 11-27-2004

FOREWORD

I've been told you never forget your first time. Your first kiss, your first love, your first car. My first time overseas was an experience that I will never forget. I experienced something that many people only read about in history books. The Second Battle of Fallujah is a watershed moment in my life. It serves as a frame of reference for my memories; before Fallujah and afterward.

I was a teenager when I raised my right hand and joined the Marine Corps. I was still a teenager when I was deployed overseas for Operation Iraqi Freedom in June 2004. Writing this book has been therapeutic for me, helping me to frame the jumbled memories that constantly replay in my mind. My experiences in Iraq are not unique among veterans of that conflict. You could probably change the names of the dusty little villages that I visited for any number of others, and any vet would recognize it. I didn't win any big medals; nothing I did was different from the thousands of others who fought alongside me.

The men who died in Bravo Company, 1st Battalion, 8th Marines deserve a special place in the hearts of all Americans. I've always wanted to tell their story, but unfortunately, God didn't grant me the gift of prose. The only way I know how to tell the world about these men is to write about the battle as I experienced it, through the eyes of a nineteen-year-old kid who was scared out of his mind.

This isn't a redemption story, and there is no silver lining or lesson to be learned. This isn't a day-by-day history of the battle either. I was not in a position to know why certain decisions were made or what units moved where. I was a young grunt armed with an M16A4 rifle and what I could carry on my back. I didn't have the perspective that the commanders had, so I can't give insight into why descisions were made. I wrote things as I remembered them.

Shortly after the battle, I wrote a timeline of events to help me keep my memory straight. I relied heavily on this timeline as well as several historical articles to piece together the big events. Like everyone else, I'm not infallible. Others may remember small details differently, as they experienced it through their own eyes.

I tried to represent things as factually as possible, but 16 years have passed since the events. At the time of the battle, I didn't feel I was in a position to judge anyone's actions or decisions. I still don't feel I have that right. I honestly believe that everyone in my unit, from the lowest PFC to the Company and Battalion Commanders, did everything to the best of their skills and abilities under challenging conditions. I have the utmost respect for my entire chain of command.

I often find myself thinking about the men who died. My thoughts are filled with a desire to know what type of men they would have become if they had not sacrificed themselves in Iraq. At times I have felt guilt that I survived when so many others did not, but such is the nature of war. I hope that by reading this you will gain some insight into how they lived and died in Fallujah.

CHAPTER 1

The first indication I had that the enemy could see me was the sound of their incoming rounds stinging in my ears. If you've never heard that before, it can be a significant emotional event. Your body instinctively flinches as your mind tries to make sense of what is happening to you. If you're lucky, you don't shit your pants once your mind begins to comprehend what's going on.

We had just stepped into the alleyway when the bullets began to whistle above our heads. I was standing next to the company executive officer, Lt. Mendez, but I couldn't see the rest of my platoon, Third Platoon, Bravo Company, 1st Battalion, 8th Marines. My mind was still trying to get its bearings when the cacophony began.

Five minutes earlier, my platoon halted in a residential courtyard off a dark Fallujah alleyway. The platoon stopped near the position of the scout sniper section. Scout snipers were trained snipers from the battalion headquarters company; at the moment, they were assigned to Bravo Company's First Platoon. First Platoon was moving ahead of Third all morning. LCpl. Jeff Walker, one of the scout snipers in the battalion, had been wounded in the arm and was awaiting a medevac.

Third Platoon stopped moving toward our objective while we waited for the evacuation. We decided to take refuge in the courtyard with the rest of the sniper section while we waited. Our objective for the day was a large community center on the north side of Fallujah. The building was part of a larger municipal district. We had been in the city for a little over 10 hours by this point.

In the courtyard, the marines in the platoon wearily plopped down where they could find space. First Platoon secured the building, so we didn't have to worry about security. Instead of staying in the courtyard with everyone else in my platoon, I went inside the house to find Walker. We had been roommates before the deployment and had become very close. I had heard he was wounded and wanted to get an update on him.

I poked around the house, looking for him. Exhausted marines from First Platoon sat in every room. An M249 machine gun from the sniper section was hammering away on the roof, but it wasn't readily apparent what they were shooting at. I asked a marine sitting at the kitchen table where Walker was, only for their medic to tell me he had been evacuated. The only signs he'd ever been there were a pile of bloody bandages and several drops of dark-red blood drying on the dusty tile floor.

I stared at the blood drying on the floor for several moments before realizing I had dawdled too long. I rushed out to the courtyard to rejoin my platoon. As I stepped into the crisp morning air, I could smell the diesel fumes of the armored vehicles. A quick glance at my watch showed it was just after 8:00 a.m. We had experienced a light rain the night before, and the ground was still wet. The storm clouds still cast gray shadows across the sky, reflected in the small pools of water that had puddled in low spots on the concrete. The ever-present sound of gunfire was getting louder.

As soon as I looked around the courtyard, I knew I was fucked. Nobody from my platoon was still there. They had left without me.

"Shit," I groaned as I began to sprint toward the entrance to the alley.

Running was no easy task, as my equipment weighed me down. My advanced combat helmet (ACH) weighed just over three and a half pounds, my interceptor body armor (IBA) weighed around sixteen pounds, and my M16A4 rifle came in at seven pounds. I also carried a black assault pack with a maul for dynamic entries, two bandoliers of 5.56 mm ammunition, one MRE ration, and an AT4 anti-tank rocket. Altogether, I had over fifty pounds of equipment strapped to my 135 lbs frame.

I'd stepped into the alley to find it empty except for our company executive officer, Lt. Mendez.

"They left me behind," I spurted out.

His response was interrupted by the crack of automatic rifle fire flying over our heads. I had never been shot at before, so the alien sound took a moment to register in my mind. The realization of what that whistling meant seemed to dawn on us both at the same time.

"Run!" he shouted as he pointed toward the end of the alleyway to indicate the direction I was to take. He ducked back into the courtyard before I could say anything in response.

I instinctively pivoted and ran after my platoon to rejoin them. In what felt like an eternity, I ran the five meters to the end of the alleyway. It intersected with a four-lane highway that bisected the city on an east-west axis. The maps we had used to plan the operation called this road Route Cathy; the Iraqis called it Fortieth Street. Route Cathy intersected with Tharthar Street, or Route Ethan. Our platoon's objective was at the intersection of Routes Cathy and Ethan.

As I turned the corner onto Route Cathy, I felt as if I had stepped into a level of Dante's *Inferno*. The air smelled of blood and burnt gunpowder. There was a marine lying facedown about ten feet in front of me. I could tell that there was gunfire all around me from the sight of bullets impacting the pavement, but for some reason, I couldn't hear anything except my labored breathing. Time seemed to slow down as I focused on the marine lying on the ground. I ran toward him, hardly conscious of the chaos surrounding me.

Within seconds I was standing next to the wounded man. Blood pooled on the ground next to him. The blood made it obvious to me that he was injured, but I was having trouble processing that his injuries were anything but minor. I reached down and grasped the green strap on the back of his body armor.

I heaved with all the strength my scrawny frame could muster. The marine was nothing but dead weight. I wasn't sure exactly what his name was; I knew him only as one of the attachments from our weapons platoon. I spotted the rest of my platoon across the street, sheltering behind a wall. I began to drag him across the street toward everyone else.

"Move your fucking legs, you stupid motherfucker!" I screamed. I still couldn't process that he was incapable of helping himself. I briefly thought it would be easier to leave him rather than continue to risk my ass dragging him across the four lanes of pavement, but I couldn't do that.

I continued to drag him along, waiting for the bullets tearing by me to find their marks. At this point, I had lost all awareness of my surroundings. My vision had narrowed, focusing only on the ground in front of me. Bullets chewed up the pavement at my feet. Each round reminded me of raindrops splashing on the pavement as they impacted. I still couldn't hear anything, and my sense of time was still warped.

I had dragged the man across the median and was halfway across the third lane when I was suddenly jerked to the ground, as if an invisible hammer had slammed into my body. I felt no pain but figured something had hit me. I later found that my gas mask had been shot; I assumed this was what had knocked me to the ground. I didn't let go of the injured marine as I fell. His heavy mass ended up on my feet. I clawed to get up again as I heard the thump of a bullet ripping into flesh. It wasn't my flesh. I knew he had been hit again, but he never moved or made a sound.

This new development caused me to promptly piss my pants. The hot urine filled my pants and ran down my leg. I began to scream obscenities at the wounded man as I scrambled to my feet. I continued to drag his dead weight toward the other side of the road. I could see my platoon sergeant, GySgt. Scott Parry, alongside other members of my platoon taking shelter behind a brick wall that ran next to our objective building. Other casualties were laid out next to the wall, awaiting the return of the medevac M113s.

I headed toward the brick wall and the relative safety it provided. I sensed a slackening in the incoming gunfire. I mentally attributed it to how close I was to the wall.

"The bastards must not be able to see us anymore," I mumbled to my silent partner. He didn't respond.

After spending a lifetime living two minutes on that street, I dropped my wounded companion in line next to another casualty, Sgt. Lonny Wells. Sgt. Wells was the squad leader for First Squad. He was lying in the dirt with blood pouring from a wound on his leg. I stared at him. His skin was an ashy color and looked like wax.

I had never seen someone die before, but I knew that I was looking at a dying man. There was no time to dwell on what I was witnessing though, I had to get cover before I joined the growing list of wounded myself. Ducking behind the wall to regain my composure, I finally regained my senses. Heavy automatic weapons fire was still filling the air as the crack of both incoming and outgoing rounds drowned out the shouts of the men around me and the groans of the wounded.

I began to take stock of my surroundings. The wall I was crouching behind protected an entrance to a large brick building. The building was the Islamic Cultural Center, a large government structure that was used as a local meeting space in more peaceful times. This imposing three-story building was my platoon's objective for the day. The mission planners had given it the lofty name of Regimental Objective One.

The men around me were desperately trying to find a way inside. The large metal doorway protected by the wall was too thick to force open. Our platoon commander, Lt. Chris Wilkens, crouched nearby. He was shouting into a radio handset, although I couldn't understand what was said over the gunfire. Next to him was the platoon radiotelephone operator (RTO), LCpl. Cullen Fitchett. Behind me, another marine was swinging a maul against the brick wall, furiously trying to make a hole we could climb through.

Wounded men were lying next to Sgt. Wells. Doc Lambotte, our platoon medic, was desperately trying to patch their wounds. I could see blood on Lambotte's pants; he had been hit as well. Sgt. Ken Hudson, the company armorer, had been shot in the hand. The bullet had gone straight through his rifle, rendering it useless. GySgt Ryan Shane, the Second Platoon Sergeant, was also lying wounded on the ground. The man I dragged across the street was lying next to Wells. I finally recognized him as LCpl. Sam Crist, an attached Mk 153 S.M.A.W. gunner from the company Weapons Platoon. Five marines were wounded crossing the street, all in a span of just over a minute.

The cultural center itself had already been secured. A Navy SEAL team from Task Force High-Value Target and a reconnaissance team from the Marine Corps' Second Reconnaissance Battalion had already secured the building. Regimental Combat Team (RCT) 7 had sent both teams the night prior as a reconnaissance element. They also served as a disruption force for our main assault force.

To the east of my position was Charlie Company's objective, the heavily fortified Al-Hadrah Mosque. We had to seize the cultural center to isolate and provide a support-by-fire position for Charlie Company's assault.

"Saxby, get inside!" bellowed SSgt. Parry. I

quickly snapped back to reality and looked at him. "Take Neely, and see if you can go around the building," he shouted.

LCpl. Charles Neely was a squad automatic rifleman (SAW) gunner in the same fire team as me. He carried a belt-fed M249 light machine gun capable of firing 850 rounds per minute at a sustained rate of fire. Neely was crouching behind the wall alongside SSgt. Parry.

"You ready?" I yelled to Neely. He nodded in the affirmative. "Go!" I cried as I began to sprint around the front side of the building.

As soon as we cleared the wall, I realized we had both made a grave mistake. The Islamic Cultural Center was a large circular building at the intersection of Cathy and Ethan. The wall we had been sheltering behind was on Route Cathy on the northern side of the building. The main entrance was on the east side of the building, directly across the street from the heavily fortified Al-Hadrah Mosque.

As we broke cover, we again were exposed to the enemy machine-gun and rifle fire from the mosque. After what seemed like another eternity, we reached the front steps. I was panting as I made the last few bounds up the steps toward the door and salvation.

As I reached the last steps, I heard the whirring sound of a turbine engine. I saw an M1A1 Abrams tank roaring south on Phase Line Ethan toward us from the corner of my eye. I quickly surmised that the reason nobody had shot us yet was that every insurgent gun in the mosque was currently blasting away at this tank.

Neely reached the door first. He grasped the worn bronzed handle and heaved with all his might. The goddamned door didn't budge.

"Fuck!" he screamed as he began to slam his fists against the door.

Miraculously, a recon marine who was inside heard our banging and unlocked the door. As we fell inside, he told us we were idiots for using the front entrance instead of the more protected rear. Neither of us cared that he was chastising us; we were just happy to be alive.

The air inside the cultural center was thick with dust. There were about thirty men already inside—a mixture of marines and a team of Navy SEALs. The concussions from the firing of their weapons had stirred up the thick dust, which hadn't had time to settle. The gunfire outside showed no signs of slackening.

"Don't go on the roof," a Navy SEAL yelled out to a group of marines who had begun climbing the stairwell. "You'll get pinned down from the sniper they got in the minaret," he cautioned. The marines quickly retreated down the stairs.

Within a few minutes, most of my platoon was inside. It was only later that I realized that Neely and I had run the wrong way. There was an entrance on the west side of the building, facing away from the mosque's heavy gunfire. We had misunderstood SSgt. Parry's directions and had unnecessarily run the gauntlet of gunfire from the wall to the front door. I wasn't having a good day.

Bravo Company had taken five casualties crossing the road to the cultural center. Sgt Wells would die from his injuries within minutes of getting into the medivac. The company began to consolidate inside. Within ten minutes of my arrival, our company commander, Capt. Read Omohundro, arrived in the building. He immediately ordered men onto the rooftop to begin suppressing the enemy positions in the Al-Hadrah Mosque.

Despite the Navy SEAL's earlier warning, I clambered up the stairs towards the rooftop. If anything, I would at least be able to breathe clean, dust-free air again. Five of us reached the rooftop, and the enemy immediately pinned us down with sniper and light machine-gun fire from the mosque's minaret. The enemy position overlooked our own and dominated us with plunging fires.

The cultural center's rooftop was like almost every other Iraqi rooftop: flat, with a three-foot-tall brick wall surrounding it. These roofs were extensions to the buildings themselves. They often had chairs and tables set up like an open-air room. The thick walls protected us from small arms fire.

I had been carrying an AT4 anti-tank rocket launcher on my shoulder the entire morning. I hurriedly unslung it and began to arm the round.

It was a long shot, but if I could somehow survive the fire long enough to get a well-aimed shot on the minaret, then maybe I could take out the enemy position. Once the rocket was cocked and armed, I placed the launcher on my shoulder and mentally prepared to expose myself.

I moved my body into a modified crouch and aimed at the minaret. Our training had taught us to check the area immediately behind the launcher to ensure nobody was there. The backblast from the rocket would kill someone if they were too close. I swung my head back to check that my backblast area was cleared. It wasn't.

Not three feet behind me was our platoon radio operator, LCpl. Fitchett. He was screaming at me not to fire, as the backblast would have killed him. I couldn't hear him over the sound of the gunfire and my nerves, but the anger was visible on his face.

I sheepishly pulled the launcher from my shoulder and un-cocked the launcher. Caution was the better part of wisdom. We collectively decided that the rooftop position was too exposed to provide accurate suppressive fire on the mosque. We beat a hasty retreat inside the building.

Once safely back within the building, we took turns firing through the windows at enemy positions in the surrounding buildings. The community center afforded us a degree of safety from the murderous fire outside. We spent the next several hours suppressing enemy positions in the area while the other infantry companies in the battalion maneuvered forward.

The battalion's mission planners assigned a platoon of four tanks to support Bravo Company throughout much of the morning. This meant that they would be under the control of Capt. Omohundro. When the Abrams tanks were outside the mosque, the volume of enemy fire tended to slacken because they would place heavy fire against any insurgent who showed himself. Unfortunately, the tanks' fuel gave them only around four hours of station time before they had to return to Camp Fallujah to refuel.

When the tanks first left the area, the intensity of the enemy fire increased significantly. Our assigned fire support team (FiST) was forced to call in artillery strikes with 155 mm shells fired from the M777 howitzers at Camp Fallujah.

Capt. Omohundro began to yell for everyone to take cover as he was authorizing a danger-close fire mission. This meant that we were inside the minimum distance required to safely fire the rounds and not receive the effects from the impacts. I soon heard the rounds come screaming in.

They sounded like freight cars flying outside before exploding with a tremendous boom. The ground shook like an earthquake with each explosion. I silently began to recite the Lord's Prayer as it felt like hell was exploding outside. The shrapnel whistled through the open-air windows of the cultural center. The shrapnel struck several marines.

I was lying on the cold concrete floor in a room with three other marines and one Navy SEAL. After the first salvo, the marine next to me looked up from the ground and toward the SEAL.

"You've seen worse, right?" he pleaded.

The SEAL's reply was not the calm reassurance of a seasoned professional we were all hoping for. "No man," he mumbled. Another round of artillery fire began to scream toward us. "You make it through this, you've seen some shit," he said through gritted teeth.

I lay there, hugging the floor, my pants still soaked in piss. I was waiting to die. I was nineteen years old and had been out of high school for only a little over a year. I couldn't help but wonder what had caused me to make the decision that had brought me to almost certain death in the city of mosques.

CHAPTER 2

My journey to Fallujah began almost thirty-four months earlier, on September 11, 2001, when I was a high school junior. I was a mediocre sixteen-year-old student at Canandaigua Academy in a sleepy little town in Upstate New York when terrorists attacked the World Trade Center.

I was old enough to understand that the America I had known in my youth would never be the same again, but I didn't yet grasp how this monumental event would change my life. There was a wave of intense patriotism following the attacks, with local homes decorated in red-white-and-blue buntings. It reminded me of a prolonged yet sad Fourth of July.

The US invasion of Afghanistan on October 7, 2001, was a memorable moment in my young mind. The thought of striking back at those who'd attacked us overjoyed me. I was also profoundly dismayed at the prospect of missing the war altogether. The news reports described nothing but the routing of the Taliban and Al Qaida forces in the region. I became convinced I was going to miss out on my chance to fight in a real war.

I enlisted in the Marines Delayed Entry Program in July 2002, immediately following my junior year of high school. My senior year of high school saw the clouds of conflict again begin to darken in media reports. I didn't question the invasion of Iraq by the US-led coalition on March 10, 2003.

The war was very unpopular in my school. On the day the invasion began, students organized a walkout in protest. These protests had little impact on me at the time. I chalked them up to over-privileged kids who didn't understand the world.

Just as with the invasion of Afghanistan, I was again excited at the chance to prove myself in war. I had this naive idea that war was going to be exciting. I had little idea of how devastating a real war could be.

My hopes for combat were dashed when President Bush landed on the USS *Abraham Lincoln* and gave his famous "Mission Accomplished" speech on May 1, 2003. I wasn't scheduled to ship out until late June. It appeared to my young mind that the US had achieved a quick victory in Iraq and that I would never get to experience the grand adventure of war.

I graduated high school on a rainy Saturday in June 2003. The next morning, I traveled with the local recruiter to the Military Entrance Processing Station (MEPS) in Buffalo, New York. On Monday morning, June 23, 2003, I began my journey in the US Marine Corps.

While waiting for my flight to Parris Island from Buffalo airport, I met another recruit with whom I would serve for my entire enlistment, Dan Bystricky. Dan was older than I was; he was the ripe old age of twenty-four when I met him. All the recruits called him an old man during our time at Parris Island; we were all so young that his twenty-four years seemed ancient.

We left Buffalo airport and flew to Dulles International in Washington, DC. We then flew on to Charleston International for our final layover. We took a small propeller-driven airplane on the last leg of our journey to the Savannah/Hilton Head Airport. I had flown only once before in my life, so this experience was memorable.

We arrived at the Savannah/Hilton Head Airport late in the evening. The sun was beginning to set as we unloaded the airplane. A gruff staff sergeant in his Class C uniform met us. It was easy to spot the recruits, as we were all young with scared looks on our faces. We were also clutching manila envelopes containing all our records. Perhaps the biggest giveaway was the stickers with our names on them that we all wore. Our recruiters had instructed us to put them on at the MEPS (Military Entrance Processing Center).

Young men and women were coming from across the country to serve in the Marines. We waited at the airport for several hours as everyone trickled in. We were taken in groups to a row of payphones and instructed to place collect calls back home. The sergeant gave us a script to read to inform our families of our safe arrivals at recruit training. The sergeant told us not to stop calling until we had reached someone. The only phone number I knew was my mom's home phone, but she didn't answer.

The sergeant in charge was getting louder in his demand that we "hurry the hell up," and I didn't want to stand out on my first day. I attempted to call home again but was unsuccessful. I couldn't just walk away as the sergeant was standing next to us to motivate our movements and ensure compliance. Feeling I had no choice, I pressed "0" for the operator and delivered the message verbatim to the perplexed woman on the other end.

Once everyone had arrived and called home, a bus drove us to Parris Island. Nobody spoke as we entered the gates to Parris Island. When the bus came to a halt outside the reception building, we all waited quietly for what was to come. The door hissed open, and a mountain of a man sauntered onto the bus. He eyeballed us for a few seconds as we dumbly stared back at him.

"Welcome to the Marine Corps Recruit Depot, South Carolina," he said. We continued to stare at him dumbly. "Now *get off my bus*!" he exploded. We all began to scramble off the bus as several more Non Commissioned Officers (NCO) in green campaign covers herded us onto yellow footprints painted on the road outside the reception center, putting everyone into a formation. The yellow footprints were symbolic of the beginning of our journey as marines.

After a forgettable introduction by the staff duty officer, we were herded through a series of stations designed to both process our files into the military system and issue the equipment necessary for recruit training. By dawn, we were dressed in digital green uniforms and had shorn heads.

Over the next few days, the clerks created our records, and everyone received immunizations and dental exams. Finally, the instructors sorted us into training platoons and companies. Bystricky and I were assigned to the Third Recruit Training Battalion, Lima Company, Platoon 3073. I had become friendly with the old man, and it was comforting to see a familiar face.

Marine Corps recruit training is a thirteen-week-long course consisting of marching, physical conditioning, drill and ceremony, and weapons qualification coupled with oppressive heat and sand fleas. We learned the fundamentals of military discipline and how to behave as marines. We didn't come out of basic training as some highly trained killers like the movies depicted. We learned fundamentals that would serve as building blocks to help us succeed in the military.

I graduated from recruit training on September 19, 2003. My parents both came down to see me graduate. Like most eighteen-year-old kids, I was proud to strut around in my uniform. I bored my parents with boot camp stories while they humored me and took me out to dinner. I weighed myself on a scale in my mom's hotel room, and I weighed a massive 117 pounds the day I graduated. The Marine Corps granted us ten days of leave before we were to report to our follow-on training.

I spent my short-lived leave period back home in Canandaigua. Soon I found myself boarding a Greyhound bus in Rochester and traveling to my follow-on training assignment, the School of Infantry (SOI) at Camp Geiger, North Carolina. At the time, SOI was fifty-two days of instruction designed to teach entry-level marines basics of infantry tactics. According to the school's curriculum, graduates were supposed to be able to "fight, survive, and win in a combat situation."

The operational demands of the Fleet Marine Forces in the fall of 2003 necessitated a shortening of our class. Instead of fifty-two days, we graduated in forty-two. We finished our training at Camp Geiger on November 26, 2003. The Marine Corps sent most of my SOI class to units stationed at nearby Camp Lejeune, North Carolina. At the time, the Marine Corps had a policy where they tried to keep recruits from the west coast in Camp Pendleton, California, and those from the east coast in Camp Lejeune. These postings were always subject to the needs of the service.

Several of us were selected to compete for a slot at the Marine Corps Force Reconnaissance Battalion in Courthouse Bay, Camp Lejeune. The design of this challenging selection course was to prepare students for the Marine Corps Basic Reconnaissance course and a follow-on position in Battalion Recon. Battalion Recon was the name given to the Division's forward reconnaissance battalion. They were tasked with acting as the eyes and ears of the Division Commander. The battalion would gather intelligence for mission planning. The Marines were in need of people, and the primary qualification in 2003 was a high score on the physical fitness test.

Bystricky and I were both selected to attend this training program, alongside about a dozen others. We were picked up outside the SOI barracks the day before Thanksgiving by a long-haired corporal driving a gray military-owned panel van. He drove us out to the Courthouse Bay barracks rooms we would call home for the next several weeks. The corporal instructed us to be in formation the following Monday morning for physical training (PT). We had four days to kill for the Thanksgiving holiday.

Bystricky and I decided to hop on a bus and head down to Myrtle Beach. This was my first holiday away from home, and I didn't want to spend it alone in the barracks. I was starting to get a little homesick. I had turned nineteen during SOI and had never been away for so long.

The weekend at Myrtle Beach was rather pathetic. Since it was Thanksgiving Day, most of the restaurants were closed by the time we got off the bus. Neither of us had a car, so we ended up eating pizza as our Thanksgiving meal. We spent the next nights in nightclubs unsuccessfully trying to pick up women. I was too young to drink legally, which thwarted much of my luck with the ladies.

On Monday, Bystricky and I were standing in formation for PT. Neither of us was too keen on going to the Basic Reconnaissance Course; our high physical fitness test scores meant we had to attend the tryouts, but it did not guarantee us a slot in recon. I felt that I would miss out on Iraq's action if I volunteered for the lengthy training pipeline necessitated by Recon. News stories were beginning to appear in the papers regarding the growing number of insurgent attacks against coalition forces. I did not have any concept that this insurgency would take years to run its course.

I lasted only about two weeks in the Reconnaissance Assessment Course before I chose to drop out. Bystricky washed out the same day as I did, just before Christmas leave. The cadre placed us in a holding squad awaiting follow-on orders to the fleet. The fleet was what we called the deployable units in the Marines. They allowed me to go home for Christmas, but I had duty on New Year's Eve. I rang in 2004 sitting as a staff duty runner in Courthouse Bay, Camp Lejeune.

After the holiday leave period, headquarters gave us our follow-on assignments. Both Bystricky and I were heading to First Battalion Eighth Marines on Camp Lejeune. We were picked up in another van by the battalion staff duty and taken to the S1 section (human resources) for processing. There were four of us, all dressed in our Class A uniforms. When the van pulled up to our new unit's headquarters area, I began to get an uneasy feeling.

The battalion headquarters was a squat brick building with several three-story barracks buildings flanking it in a U shape. These barracks looked like a seedy, run-down motel, with rooms opening to long catwalks. Hanging over the railings of these catwalks were marines. These men began to jeer and shout at us, taunting us with shouts of "Fresh meat!" and calling us *boots*.

A *boot* was a derogatory word in the Marine Corps. It was a word I came to know all too well. A *boot* was someone who was inexperienced and had never deployed. Boots were lower than dog shit in the Marine Corps hierarchy.

Our escort hurriedly ushered us into the battalion office and the S1 shop. S1 shops were run by clerks who managed all personnel actions within the unit. Each battalion and higher-level headquarters had one, and they functioned as the commander's human resources section.

An uninterested desk clerk gave us our company assignments. Bystricky and I were both assigned to Bravo Company, along with another Recon washout. His name was LCpl. Jeff Walker and he was assigned as my roommate in the barracks. The S1 clerk assigned Walker and me to Third Platoon while Bystricky went to Second.

By the time we got through with the S1 clerk, it was after 1700. We were given keys to our new rooms and dismissed. Thankfully, most of the marines had left their catwalk perches by the time we got out of S1. We were able to get to our rooms relatively unscathed and unmolested.

CHAPTER 3

"Get up, boot!" the barracks charge of quarters (CQ) NCO gruffly shouted as he slammed his fists against the door. "Get outside and police call." He turned and headed down the balcony toward his next victims.

"What the fuck?" I groaned as I glanced at my watch. It was a quarter to six in the morning. The barracks staff duty NCO had chosen my room to conduct the morning police call, or trash pickup. I could hear Walker stumbling out of bed through the darkness on the other side of the room.

Within minutes we got dressed in our green shorts and T-shirts. I had been in 1st Battalion, 8th Marines for two weeks now. Being a boot meant that I was constantly selected for menial labor, such as conducting this morning's police call. Walker and I shuffled out into the retreating darkness. I could see the New River off in the distance. The water was illuminated by the sun, which was just beginning to appear above the horizon.

I could hear the other boots coming out of their rooms around me as I made my way to the courtyard. Our mission was to pick up discarded cigarette butts. Around ten of us lined up in the grass at the far edge of the building. The NCO who had so rudely interrupted our slumber stood on the second-floor balcony, indifferently eyeing us. He was slowly dragging on the cigarette clutched between his lips.

"Well, let's get a fucking move on," he bellowed.

We began to shuffle over the ground. The constant tread of marines walking over it had worn down the grass. The exposed sandy soil created a fine dust that coated everything. We walked with bent-over backs, sifting through the grass and sand with our feet to find and remove any cigarette butts or trash. After we went from one end of the building to the other, we stopped and turned around. All eyes turned toward the duty NCO, who was just finishing his cigarette from his balcony perch. He took one final drag on the cigarette before flicking it off the balcony into our freshly cleaned dirt.

"Looks good," he mumbled as he turned and walked away.

Released from our current duty, I looked around to see where else I could help. Other marines were finishing up various chores, so it looked like I was off the hook. I went back to my room to get ready for the day.

The Marine Corps would graduate SOI classes and send most of the graduates to the same unit in large groups. The influx of personnel creates a cohort within each battalion filled with marines who entered and subsequently left the service around the same timeframe. First Battalion Eighth Marines had just returned from a deployment on a Marine Expeditionary Unit (MEU) rotation. During this deployment, they had participated in the initial invasion of Iraq.

I had the misfortune of arriving in one of the first waves of replacements after their return. All the junior NCOs in my new battalion were combat veterans of the Battle of Mosul during the summer of 2003. I was unsure if their rough treatment stemmed from a genuine disdain for us greenhorn boots or if they were trying to harden us up to face the difficult challenges that they knew lay ahead.

Back in my room, I got changed for our morning PT session. After conducting my hygiene routine and getting ready, I had about ten minutes before the first formation. I headed over to the quad, where we formed up, and found my place. I was assigned to Bravo Company, Third Platoon, Second Squad, Bravo Team. We lined up by platoon. Each platoon formation consisted of three squads lined up in rows. The man on the farthest left of each squad was the squad leader. Based on our authorized military table of organization and equipment, the squad leader was supposed to be a sergeant. We rarely had the luxury of someone with that much experience.

To the squad leader's right was the Alpha Team leader, usually a corporal. Next to him was his fire team, consisting of three other marines: an automatic rifleman who was assigned the M249 SAW and two riflemen armed with M16A4s. The next four marines in line were the Bravo Team with the same composition. They were supposed to be followed by a Charlie Team, but Third Platoon didn't have the manpower to fill the third team.

Each company consisted of three rifle platoons and one weapons platoon. The weapons platoon was composed of machine gunners, mortarmen, and infantry assault men. The infantry assault men were specially trained to assault fortified targets with rockets, demolitions, and breaching techniques. These marines were armed with the MK153 Shoulder-Launched Multipurpose Assault Weapon (SMAW), a portable rocket system.

I quickly found my place in the formation. My team leader was Cpl. Wayne Bowman, a wiry twenty-one-year-old from Watertown, Tennessee. Next to me in formation was our SAW gunner, PFC Charles Neely from Georgetown, Kentucky. Rounding out our team was LCpl. David Houck, from Mount Ulla, North Carolina. Houck and Bowman were both veterans of Mosul, while Neely and I were fresh out of basic.

The Alpha Team leader was Cpl. Robbie Landers from South Boston, Massachusetts. He would continuously deride us in his thick Boston accent. Landers was incredibly hard on Neely. Alpha Team consisted of LCpl. David Maxey as his M249 SAW gunner and PFC Mike Fonda and PFC Sammy Gravano as riflemen. Landers and Maxey were both veterans of Mosul.

Our squad leader was one of the youngest squad leaders in the company. Sgt. Allen Hayden was a tall, lanky man from Immokalee, Florida, who had come through the ranks with Bowman and Landers. I sometimes thought they used this personal relationship to get away with things. Despite this, Hayden took his job seriously and tried his best to train us. He wasn't a hard-ass like other squad leaders in the company. Instead of yelling, he would often talk to us as an older brother might.

Typically PT formations consisted of either a platoon or squad run followed by calisthenics. The company gunnery sergeant or company first sergeant would get accountability for everyone before turning the formation over to the platoon sergeants. Today was different, though.

We all snapped to the position of attention as the first sergeant took control of the formation. 1st Sgt. Ronald Whittington was an imposing marine with a constant scowl on his face. Junior marines like me steered clear of him whenever he came around. We were all afraid of feeling his wrath.

After receiving the morning report from each of the platoon sergeants, he instructed the company to stand at ease.

"Devil Dogs, the CO (commanding officer) is waiting on more specifics, but be prepared to deploy to Iraq in June." He said. Devil dogs is a common name for marines in the Marine Corps. It refers to a nickname given to the marines by the Germans in WW1. The story claims that marine's fought like dogs from hell.

1st Sgt. Whittington spoke of the upcoming training regime we would all have, but I wasn't particularly interested. My mind remained fixated on the news that I would soon deploy. When he finished, he dismissed the platoons to conduct PT on their own.

I was ecstatic. I would finally have a chance to get in on the action. After PT, I ran into Bystricky walking toward the barracks.

"You ready for this shit?" I asked him, referring to the impending deployment.

"Hell yeah" was his enthusiastic response.

I spent the next several days with my head in the clouds, daydreaming about how I would win medals and impress people back home with my war stories. I began to pay more attention to the news articles coming out of Iraq. Things seemed to be progressing well. Sure, there was some minor fighting, but from my estimation, it looked as if things were going in the US's favor, and I was worried I would miss out on the actual fighting.

Sgt. Hayden and the other NCOs in my squad began to take more of an interest in our training. It would be several weeks before we started our first company-level training events. We took the time to work on our readiness, focusing on rifle marksmanship, conditioning drills, and patrolling. Our daily focus was on team- and squad-level tactics.

Houck broke his arm one weekend, so he couldn't participate in all our training. I will never forget the company gunnery sergeant screaming at him for showing up to formation wearing a neon-pink cast on his arm. Because of this injury, he missed out on a lot of the individual training we conducted.

The armorer issued me a brand-new rifle, the M16A4. This rifle had a stiffened barrel and a Picatinny rail system allowing for attachments such as tactical lights and hand grips. My rifle's serial number was 10155072. I would end up carrying this same rifle for my entire time in the Marine Corps.

CHAPTER 4

Our first company-level training exercise was in early March 2004. It took place at Camp Lejeune's urban training complex, or MOUT facility. MOUT is an acronym for military operations in urban terrain. It describes how marines and soldiers fight in built-up urban areas.

We rode out to the training area in large M1078 Light Medium Tactical Vehicles (LMTVs)—specifically, we were in five-ton cargo trucks. The trucks stopped just short of the training area, and we dismounted onto the dusty road. I quickly pushed out into the tree line on the side of the road and took a knee, facing out towards the woods to pull security. The weight of my heavy rucksack pressed against my shoulders. I had my body armor on, with a ceramic armored plate on the front and the back. The weight of the ruck pressing against the plate felt like a knife sticking into my shoulders. I could already feel the sweat forming on my back, and beads of it were fogging up my thick glasses.

I glanced back toward the trucks every few moments. My head was supposed to be on a swivel, continually scanning from left to right. All the other men in my squad were in similar positions. Once we had dismounted from the truck, we'd fanned out in a 360-degree pattern. The SAW from each team faced down opposite ends of the long axis of the dirt road. This formation gave us all-around security with our most-casualty-producing weapon on the most likely approach routes.

After sitting on my knees for what felt like ten minutes, my leg began to go numb. I glanced back toward the road. Sgt. Hayden was talking with Bowman and Landers. Finally, Landers stood up and motioned for his team to follow. He silently gave the hand signal for a wedge formation. The Alpha Team men rose and silently followed him in the diamond-shaped wedge formation. Maxey took a position on the far left of the formation, and Gravano took the lead, with Fonda to his right.

Sgt. Hayden followed the Alpha Team by about fifteen meters; then, Bowman gave us the signal to move. Houck was still recovering from his recently removed arm cast, so Bowman took point. Our formation was the mirror image of Alpha's with Neely on the right flank and myself on the left.

We moved slowly through the tree line; our eyes were continually swiveling, scanning for any signs of movement. The sunlight filtered through the dense tree canopy. It cast shadows over us as we crept through the underbrush. Suddenly I saw Bowman's hand shoot into the air, palm extended in the hand signal to freeze. I stopped my movement and stood like stone. After ten seconds, I dropped to a knee behind a tree. I could see from the bright sunlight ahead that we had reached the edge of the tree line. Our training objective was to patrol to the edge of the MOUT site, then secure one of the buildings on the perimeter of the village.

Sgt. Hayden emplaced Landers's team in a support-by-fire position at the edge of the tree line. This technique allowed Landers and his men to fire on the building while Sgt. Hayden and the rest of the squad maneuvered onto the flank of the building. They would then cease their fire once we got to a predetermined point, usually fifteen degrees off the building.

The crackling of gunfire announced our presence in the area. We were armed with blank ammunition, which allowed us to fire without any real effects. Sgt. Hayden began to yell at us to move faster. We stood and raced toward the clearing. Our formation went from a wedge shape into a file as we broke the tree line. We ran toward the side of the building as Landers's team continued to suppress.

Sgt. Hayden threw out a piece of a neon-orange VS-17 panel attached to a rock. This panel was designed to signal aircraft flying overhead, but he used it as an easily identifiable signal for Landers to stop firing. The signal would avoid having us maneuver directly into the fire of those in the support-by-fire position.

My breathing was labored as I reached the edge

of the building. I stacked up on the wall immediately behind Bowman. His weapon remained trained on the doorway—what we called the *fatal funnel*. Doors were funnels because everyone had to go through them to enter a room, making them easy to target. Neely was immediately behind me in the stack.

Neely squeezed my thigh, giving me the signal that he was ready; I reached out and tapped Bowman. He nodded, telling me he understood. The muscles in my body strained in anticipation. Bowman rocked back on his heels before springing forward into the doorway. He button hooked to the left; I followed. I momentarily lost my sight as I ran from the bright outdoors into the building's darkness. I came to a stop next to Bowman on the left side of the room. Sweat dripped from my brow and into my eyes; my heart was racing after all the exertion. I was excited to be training for war in the Marines.

As my eyes adjusted to the darkness of the room, I was able to focus on a lone figure standing in the corner. The man's arms were crossed, and he was staring right through me.

"Well, you're dead, Saxby," he said. His eyes never left me. "You know why, right?" he asked.

"No, Sergeant," I stammered in reply.

"You were supposed to go opposite the number one man; instead, you followed him. That means nobody cleared the right side of the room until you two were already committed," he lectured.

"That means you're fucking dead."

Sgt. Lonny Wells was the squad leader for First Squad. He was the second-oldest marine in the platoon and had a wealth of experience. Sgt. Hayden had asked him to evaluate our entry into the building. I had failed his evaluation. The elation I had felt only minutes prior quickly faded as I pondered how I had let Wells down.

The rest of the day consisted of each squad in the platoon working on our room-clearing techniques. The entire company was out working on room-clearing at the squad level. By the time night fell, I was exhausted. Unfortunately, there would be little rest in store for me.

The coming darkness meant we had to practice what we had learned during the day again. Only now under limited visibility using a pair of AN/PVS-7Ds. These were binocular night vision goggles (NVGs) attached to my Kevlar helmet through a hinged elbow at the front. Peering through the NVGs cast everything in an eerie green glow.

The PVS-7s gave me no depth perception. The NVGs made navigating the narrow hallways and tight corners very difficult. My movements were like those of an intoxicated man. I clumsily tried to maintain muzzle awareness without tripping over my own feet. I ended up walking into more than a few walls as we practiced our craft.

The more experienced marines acted as guides. Cpl. Landers helped me adjust the padding in my Kevlar to alleviate the piercing headache caused by the prolonged weight of the NVGs pressing into my forehead. Houck showed us how to aim our rifles by pointing the index finger of our left hand in the direction of our targets. The theory behind this technique was that your body always knows where your fingers are. The left hand was closest to the barrel (for a right-handed person), so you could easily point at your target. At the close ranges of house-to-house fighting, the M16 was a point-and-shoot weapon. The other marines' experiences fighting in Mosul during the initial invasion were invaluable as we began to form a cohesive fighting force.

After running through several house-clearing scenarios, we moved out into the streets to rehearse patrolling in an urban environment. Instead of the V-shaped fire team wedge formation we had utilized in the trees, we used a column formation. A column formation alternated marines on either side of the road in a long file. There was a forty-five-degree offset between marines. The offset kept the point man out of the center of the street and allowed us to use the buildings' walls as cover.

We practiced a technique called *pieing off* whenever we encountered doorways and windows. This technique involved pointing our muzzles at the far end of the opening and then shifting toward the end opposite your travel direction. The field of fire of your muzzle created a pie shape as you scanned the room. This technique allowed us to visually clear places without having to expose ourselves by entering them.

Unlike patrolling in a woodland environment, urban settings had multiple levels. These levels meant that one must continuously be scanning. It also forced the squad to assign different sectors that each man must cover. There were five levels to an urban battlespace.

The highest level was the airspace overhead. Airspace was important to the patrol leader because vital air support and indirect fire traveled through it to support operations. Of more importance to the rifle platoons and squads were the super surfaces (rooftops), the intrasurface (interiors), the ground-level surfaces, and the subsurface (underground). These areas comprised the battlespaces in which all our operations physically occurred.

Patrolling through the streets of the MOUT facility at night was a challenging experience for our untested squad. I was both physically and mentally exhausted from the long day of training. At every halt, I would take a knee and peer off into the green landscape provided by the NVGs.

I felt a tap on my shoulder. I shook my head; I must have fallen asleep. I looked up to see Bowman standing over me.

"Let's move," he whispered.

I looked ahead and saw that Landers's team had already started to move on. I staggered to my feet and began to follow. We patrolled to a building that was supposed to represent a hotel in the fictitious training town. I entered the building and found that the rest of the platoon had already occupied it. Third Squad was ordered to a small room on the second floor.

"This is going to be our base of operations for the rest of the week," Sgt. Hayden informed us. "I need two marines on watch; everyone else, get some sleep."

Thankfully I wasn't selected to stand watch. I lay on the floor, propped up against my rucksack, and fell fast asleep. We spent the next three days rehearsing our squad patrolling and room clearing. Each day Sgt. Hayden introduced an additional level of complexity into the mix. We slowly became a more proficient squad.

The company headquarters (HQ) section served as the opposing forces (OPFOR) for the exercise. Company HQ section consists of the arms room clerk, the training NCO, a communications NCO, and a supply clerk. This section is responsible for the administrative functions of an infantry company. While serving as the OPFOR, they would shoot at us from windows and doorways, forcing us to react. This training forced the squad to act more cohesively. After three days of continuous patrols, I could discern who each squad member was just by watching them walk in the darkness. I didn't need to see their faces.

In the final two days of the exercise, we focused on platoon-level training. We drew new upper receivers from the supply sergeant for our last mission. The new uppers we received fired a 9 mm paint round. Those Simuniton rounds left welts when they hit, enabling better training by allowing marines to feel the effects of their decisions physically. We were also issued a patrol order for the final training event. Our mission was to clear a large three-story building at the village's edge. Each platoon was tasked with providing a marine to augment the headquarters section as OPFOR. Houck served as our contribution to the OPFOR, as he was still on light duty.

The commander assigned each platoon a subobjective, which would allow the company to seize their overall objective. He tasked First Platoon with capturing buildings around the target to isolate our company objective. They would then serve as a reserve force for the commander. Second Platoon was tasked with seizing a foothold in the building. Third Platoon would then pass through Second to clear the rest of the building. The weapons platoon was broken up into sections to augment the three rifle platoons.

We were last in the order of movement. While we patrolled the village streets toward our objective, gunfire broke the silence. First Platoon was in heavy contact with OPFOR on their objective. We began to increase our pace. Third Squad was in the platoon trail, so I was one of the last marines in the formation.

The crackle of gunfire died down for several

minutes before picking up again. The gunfire indicated that Second Platoon was beginning to assault the objective. To my left, I could see the lights of First Platoon in the buildings. They were conducting sensitive site exploitation and establishing a casualty-collection point. Shouting mixed with heavy gunfire was resonating from the objective building.

Second Platoon was heavily engaged with OPFOR in the building. Third Platoon waited outside for the signal to enter.

"Let's move!" shouted Sgt. Hayden.

My squad stood up and raced toward the entrance to the building. Second Platoon had marked our entry point with a glowing green chem light tied to an orange VS-17 panel. When I entered the building, the gunfire was deafening. Marines were lying and sitting down all over the place. The sim rounds had hit these men, and the corpsman had assessed them as casualties.

I raced upstairs, following the rest of my platoon. As I rounded the first turn in the stairway, I saw Bystricky sitting on the floor with a sour look on his face. The orange blobs of paint peppering his chest showed me he wasn't having as much fun as I was.

I ran past him and found myself on the second floor, in a long hallway with a stairwell on each end. Rooms ran the length of both sides of the hallway. The OPFOR had barricaded themselves behind the doors to those rooms and were extracting a heavy toll on the company.

As I went from room to room, I became separated from the rest of my squad. I found myself with two members of Second Squad—PFC Mike Rodriguez and PFC Jeffrey Holmes. Rodriguez was a Coast Guard brat who had always been friendly with me. Holmes was a tall kid from White River Junction, Vermont. He was outspoken and well liked in the platoon. Both were boots like me. We stacked on a room together and began to enter as practiced.

We had just passed through the doorway when shots rang out from behind us in an adjacent doorway. Holmes was shot by an OPFOR who had taken up a position in an adjoining room. Rodriguez and I quickly fired at the shape in the darkness.

"Fuck, I'm out," the shape yelled. It was the company radio operator, a member of the headquarters platoon. Rodriguez and I left Holmes and continued clearing. We made our way up the stairwell to the third floor. The defenders had extracted a heavy toll on the platoons. The commander called in First Platoon to reinforce. Packed in the stairs with us were the remnants of Second and Third Platoons. Above the din of the gunfire, I could hear Houck laughing and shouting. He seemed to be having a grand old time shooting the company.

An NCO from First Platoon, CPL Nate Anderson, took control of us in the stairwell. All my NCOs were either a casualty or still in other parts of the building, clearing it out.

"When I tell you to, I want you to pop out and secure that hallway; got it?" Anderson told us. I nodded my understanding and moved into position.

"Move!" he shouted. I kneeled out into the hallway with my rifle pointed toward the end.

A sharp pain in my arm told me I had leaned out too far. Two more hits in my chest confirmed my suspicions. I heard Houck shout out to me.

"You're out, Saxby," he laughed.

"I know. Fuck," was all I could muster. I sat back down in the hallway as the rest of the company finished clearing the building.

A few minutes later, I was carried/dragged to a room serving as our casualty-collection point (CCP). The room was bursting with laughing marines. The smiles on our faces gave away how much fun we were having. The entire attack had been a carefully orchestrated game of paintball.

I surveyed the mass of men in the CCP with me and thought how terrible the cost of seizing this building had been. A small group of around ten OPFOR had "killed or wounded" around eighty men. I sat there and thought how lucky we had been; it was all just a drill. I consoled myself by thinking that large-scale urban combat didn't happen very often.

CHAPTER 5

Shortly after returning to the garrison from our first field operation, we received a new company commander. Capt. Read Omohundro was a mustang officer who had fought in the Gulf War. A *mustang* was a prior-enlisted marine who later became a commissioned officer. He would be our commander throughout our upcoming deployment to Iraq.

Under Capt. Omohundro's guidance, the company conducted another weeklong training event. Instead of going to different training sites, we instead stayed on the Camp Lejeune main post and used the local buildings. We turned an unused base gym into a forward operating base (FOB). That was where the company headquartered itself while the platoons and squads conducted patrols through the local area. We continued to refine our techniques and began to mesh into a more cohesive team.

In early April, we finally got a platoon commander. 2nd Lt. Christopher Wilkens was an Ithaca College graduate. His stocky build made him look like a linebacker. My first introduction to Lt. Wilkens was when we were standing in our morning PT formation. Sgt. Hayden informed us the new lieutenant would conduct a walk-through of the barracks with GySgt. Parry.

"How's it feel to know you've been promoted more times than the boot lieutenant?" Landers asked me as we prepared for the walk-through. It appeared as if his disdain for new members of the platoon wasn't just restricted to the junior enlisted. I didn't give him a reply.

A half-hour later, Walker and I were standing outside our room, ready for the inspection. GySgt. Parry and 2nd Lt. Wilkens turned the corner and headed straight for us.

"Ah-ten-hut!" shouted Walker as we both snapped to the position of attention.

"At ease," ordered Wilkens. GySgt. Parry walked into the room to inspect it while the new lieutenant stayed outside with us. He made small talk with us for a minute. Lt. Wilkens seemed as nervous as we were. He looked to be just a few years older than I was. It must have been difficult to be thrust into such a position of responsibility at such a young age.

GySgt. Parry walked out of the room, apparently satisfied. They began to walk toward the next room when Parry stopped. He turned around and said, "We're getting a new corpsman today. I'm putting him in your room." He then turned and walked away.

HN "Doc"Joel Lambotte was the new platoon medic. He was originally from Topeka, Kansas. Both Walker and I took an immediate liking to him, and we soon became close friends.

Within a week of the new arrivals to the platoon, we shipped off to our final pre-deployment exercise. The Marines flew the entire battalion out to March Air Reserve Base in Riverside, California. The base had recently shut down its on-post housing, which the Air Force had scheduled for demolition. We could use the area as a training site before the start of the demolition.

The focus of the training in California was company-level operations. The company occupied an abandoned community center to use as a FOB. The OPFOR that we faced consisted of marines brought back on active duty from the inactive reserve. These men had gotten out of the Marines, then had been recalled from their civilian lives to help us prepare for Iraq. They did not seem happy to be there.

Civilian role players were brought in to play the part of both Iraqi civilians and the military. Platoon missions consisted of meetings with these villagers as well as joint patrols. We practiced reacting to contact, cordon and searches, and company attacks. One mission stands out from all the rest: a company-sized attack on an OPFOR stronghold.

First Platoon was tasked as the isolation element, meaning they moved in first and surrounded the objective building, ensuring nobody got into the area. Third Platoon was the support-by-fire and inner-cordon element. Our mission was to be prepared to suppress the assault element's objective and ensure that nobody left the target area. Second Platoon was the assault force, and the weapons platoon was broken down to support the other platoons. Once Second established security, they would be the ones to move in and seize the objective.

The mission initially went according to plan. 2nd Lt. Andrew Eckert, the First Platoon commander, was able to get his marines into position with little opposition. Lt. Wilkens was likewise able to get the inner-cordon and support-by-fire positions established. We could see the OPFOR moving around on the objective.

Second Platoon under 2nd Lt. Steve Berch moved in to assault the objective. They did not fare as well as their sister platoons and took several casualties. The commander called in Third Platoon to help move these casualties to a nearby helicopter landing zone (HLZ). My squad went with Lt. Wilkens to help with the medevac. Bowman told me to help move their platoon sergeant, Gunnery Sergeant Ryan Shane. Shane was a mountain of a man, and it took six of us to drag him to the HLZ. Due to his size, moving him was a significant emotional and physical undertaking for us, and it took everything we had. Little did we know that this situation would repeat itself in several months.

Once we got to the HLZ, we set up security and waited for the medevac helicopter. Lt. Wilkens made radio contact with the pilot and advised him he would throw a smoke grenade to mark our location. I watched him reach into his assault pack and remove the smoke grenade. He pulled the pin and heaved the grenade into the field.

The smoke began to billow as hot flames shot out the back of the M18 smoke grenade. The fire quickly ignited the dry California grass. Within a minute, the flames were spreading as a small brush fire began to consume the field. The flames forced the helicopter to another HLZ while we started to try and fight the growing conflagration futilely. Soon, range control brought in the local fire department. They were able to bring the fire under control. We all got a chuckle out of the entire incident.

On our last night in California, we were finally allowed off the post. Lambotte and I went with PFC Lopez Hernandez and PFC Bradley Parker to a local mall. Parker and Hernandez were members of First and Second Squads, respectively. The entire company was under orders to abstain from alcohol during the evening.

When we returned to base, we found that we were the only marines to adhere to the no-drinking order. Bowman and I had to help hold Houck up in the accountability formation because he was so intoxicated. He probably would have lost rank if someone had caught him. It was the only time I ever saw him drunk.

We all survived the evening's festivities with nothing more than a hangover. We flew back to

Camp Lejeune. The last hurdle we all had to overcome before our Iraq adventure was pre-deployment leave. Everyone got two weeks of leave. I drove home to Canandaigua with PFC Kyle Gilg, another marine from the platoon. He lived a few towns over in Geneseo, New York. I dropped him off at his parent's house and headed for home.

I spent the leave period trying to pretend that I wasn't about to deploy to Iraq. I chased girls (rather unsuccessfully) and hung out with my friends. During this time, I also read the novel *Johnny Got His Gun* by Dalton Trumbo. I prayed I wouldn't share a fate with the book's protagonist, who was injured and couldn't communicate with the outside world. It was challenging to maintain my focus while at home.

The two-week break flew by, and I soon found myself back at Camp Lejeune. The next several weeks consisted of loading containers and endless equipment inspections. We soon had nothing to do but wait for our flight overseas.

Shortly after returning to Camp Lejeune, Lt. Wilkens brought us all into the company conference room. Insurgents had just decapitated an American journalist by the name of Nicholas Berg in Iraq. They had released a gruesome video depicting their vile actions. Lt. Wilkens wanted us to see what type of men we were going to be facing. As I watched the man's tragedy unfold on the screen, I thought back to Trumbo's novel. I couldn't help but wonder how I would fare in the coming storm.

CHAPTER 6

We left Camp Lejeune in Blue Bird buses. The radio on the bus blasted "No Sleep till Brooklyn" by the Beastie Boys as we pulled away from the battalion area. We rode to the airfield on Cherry Point, North Carolina. The plane took off in the early morning of June 23, 2004. A year to the day from my entry into the Marine Corps. I sat between Houck and Neely on the flight over. We flew from Cherry Point to the airport in Bangor, Maine. We stayed in Bangor for around an hour so the plane could refuel before heading to our next stop in Frankfurt, Germany.

Over twenty-four hours after leaving North Carolina, we found ourselves preparing to land in an airfield near Camp Buehring, Kuwait. The sun was setting on the airfield as the plane came to a stop. I stepped out of the plane and onto the stairs leading to the tarmac. I felt the hot blast of air from the engines in my face. As I got to the bottom of the stairs and began to file off the flight line, I realized it wasn't the engine blast I was feeling. The hot blast of air was from the desert wind blowing in my face.

The heat in Kuwait was hotter than anything I had ever experienced before. We shuffled off the flight line toward a large tent in which we were going to be briefed. We walked past a large wooden box packed with Meals Ready-to-Eat (MREs). The flight line personnel instructed us to each grab a meal to consume during the in-briefs.

I walked inside the tent and found a chair. I opened my MRE and pulled out a bag of crushed pineapples. Hungrily I tore open the bag and dipped my spoon in. When I popped the spoonful into my mouth, I found that the intense heat from the sun had cooked the entire pack. Realizing that this would probably be all I had to eat for a while, I continued to eat the warm, soggy mess.

The briefing itself was the usual military death by PowerPoint. A list of rules, customs, courtesies, and a basic orientation to Camp Buehring and Camp New York. We were also given a rough timeline of how long we could expect to wait before we were in Iraq. We would stay in Kuwait for several days waiting on equipment to arrive before taking a military flight into Al Asad, Iraq.

After the briefings, we made our way outside into the darkness. We had to load our rucks and duffel bags into a waiting cargo truck. Once we finished loading bags, we piled into buses driven by local drivers. The radio was playing on the bus, providing me my first taste of Arabic music. Listening to the unfamiliar music drove home to me that I was no longer in the US. During the bus ride, I listened to Sgt. Wells talking to Lcpl. Jeff Holmes and Kyle Gilg.

"I think we'll all end up getting Humanitarian

Service Medal for this; I doubt any of you will get your Combat Action Ribbon," Wells told them. "The heavy fighting's pretty much all over—just sporadic attacks here and there."

I sat silently and stared out the window into the darkness, listening to the unfamiliar music. I hoped I hadn't missed all the action, even though the thought of fighting was somewhat terrifying.

We arrived at Camp New York and moved into a large tent. The entire camp consisted of rows of civilian tents, almost resembling a circus. The chow hall was another large tent run by civilian contractors. We slept on green military-issued cots for the two days we were there.

We tried to limit our movements during the daytime due to the oppressive heat. After two days, we took civilian buses back to the airport to board a C-130 airplane for our flight to Iraq. Most of the other marines fell asleep on the plane. Men and rucksacks were packed so tight into the aircraft that I couldn't move my legs. Cpl. Straub, a team leader from First Squad, fell asleep on my legs. I alternated my gaze from the rocky landscape visible outside a small window to the giant ball of snot hanging from the tip of Straub's nose. I watched my first sunset in Iraq from the back of that airplane. It was pitch black when we landed at Al Asad Airbase. The date was June 27, 2004.

I was fully expecting to step off the plane into a hostile war zone with blackout lights and marines in full body armor. Instead, I saw marines with reflective belts around their chests working under bright floodlights without their weapons. My initial impression of Al Asad Airbase was that it resembled a peacetime airbase in the middle of the desert.

We were bused from the airfield to a row of tents identical to what we had seen in Kuwait. As we drove through the base, I was amazed at how cozy the life of the POGs (a derogative term for non-infantry types) in the rear areas was. We also called them Fobbits, a mixture of the word hobbits and the term FOB. A FOB is an acronym for a forward operating base. Marines were riding bicycles through the base complex, and there were locals selling coffee from the back of food carts.

We soon got settled into our temporary living quarters. I ended up on an old, sweat-stained military cot, where I curled up and tried to sleep. Sleep did not come easily, but eventually, I drifted off.

I awoke early the following morning and went to explore my surroundings with Lambotte. We were billeted in a small cluster of tents. Each tent was serviced with a large air conditioner and housed one platoon. The chow hall was a large semi-permanent structure set off to the side of the living tents.

There was a large area of around one hundred portable toilets, which was the only latrine facility available. The tents and the chow hall were serviced by contracting companies from the States. The latrines were serviced by a local national with a dilapidated tanker truck.

There was a Post Exchange (PX) across the post, a twenty-minute walk from where we were living. The PX was run by the military. Lambotte and I decided to walk there. On the way, we passed a large clamshell-shaped building that housed the battalion maintenance sections and served as a large motor pool.

The PX carried all of the creature comforts you could expect to find in the States. They had selections of the latest CDs, cold drinks, and candy. We bought ice-cold sports drinks. Instead of real change, we were given cardboard disks with the denomination of the coin they represented. The cashier said these were cheaper than shipping real coins. We could redeem the disks at any US commissary for face value.

We returned to our tents and were quickly put to work downloading our platoon's new-to-us equipment. It was costly to outfit every unit with new equipment in the States and then ship the unit and its equipment to Iraq. The military would just leave equipment in Iraq to reduce costs and distribute limited supplies of the latest equipment in the right locations. Units would rotate in and fall in on the equipment left by the outgoing unit.

Our platoon's theater property consisted of an HMMWV truck, ammunition stocks, and other specialized equipment the battalion may have required. The vehicles were all labeled US Army on the insides and were of the M038A1 variants. Each platoon received a truck. The company commander received an M1151 truck with a blue force tracker (BFT) system. The BFT allowed him to communicate with adjacent and higher echelon units and see their physical locations on the map in real-time.

Al Asad Airbase was also the location for our higher headquarters, RCT 7. Over the next several days, orders flowed from RCT 7 to the battalion, then down to the company and the platoon. At the squad level, we waited for orders and prepared to move when called.

We re-zeroed our rifles on a makeshift rifle range. Supply issued everyone with a basic combat load of 240 rounds of 5.56 mm ball ammunition. M249 gunners received 1,000 rounds of 5.56 mm linked. Sgt. Hayden took us on practice patrols both around the tents and in an adjacent field by the motor pool in our spare time. There was an abandoned Iraqi bunker near the clamshell building, which we used to practice MOUT in.

On July 3, 2004, we planned to move from Al Assad Airbase to our new home in Al Anbar Providence. The day prior, Lt. Wilkens briefed the platoon on our new mission. The battalion was taking over security in the city of Haditha. Headquarters Company was stationed in the Haditha Dam complex on Lake Qadisiyah on the Euphrates River. Bravo Company would be detailed to guard an abandoned ammunition supply point (ASP) called ASP Wolf. The depot had been a storage area for Saddam Hussein's army before the initial invasion in March 2003. When the US took control of the area, we had tried to destroy the ordinance by blowing it up. The contractors hired to destroy the munitions had done it improperly, and now artillery rounds and other unexploded munitions were lying unguarded in the middle of the ruined complex.

I was detailed to drive one of the HMMWVs out there. There were very few licensed HMMWV drivers in the company at this point in the rotation, so I was tasked with driving vehicles for other squads and platoons. There were only enough vehicles to move one platoon at a time, so we had to make several trips. First Platoon was assigned to occupy ASP Wolf first, and then the trucks would drive back and get Third and Weapons. Second would stay at Al Asad for several more weeks.

We staged the vehicles in the motor pool on Al Asad on the night of July 3. Early in the morning on the Fourth of July, our convoy departed. My truck had two wooden benches running along the sides of the bed, where the marines rode. There was no turret; the only protection was a marine standing in the back with his SAW bipods resting on the truck's roof.

The platoon commander gave us a pre-convoy brief, and then we conducted pre-mission rehearsals. The entire trip would take around an hour to complete. We would head north on the road called Route Gold before turning west at a police checkpoint. We would then take Route Bronze until we reached ASP Wolf. After the brief, we rehearsed actions in contact and rollover drills.

If we took contact, we would push through the enemy kill zone. If we had to dismount, the trucks would stop in a herringbone formation, and the marines in the back would dismount and establish security. The gunners on the trucks would establish a support by fire so the dismounts could maneuver.

After several iterations of rehearsals, we were ready to set out. In the grand scheme of things, my job was easy. Maintain a one-hundred-meter dispersion with the truck in front of me, and drive in the center of the road to avoid improvised explosive devices (IEDs).

We drove through a C-wire arranged in a serpentine pattern to get through the gate of Al Asad. C-wire is barbed wire which is coiled into a circle. It was used to form protective barriers. I had to weave the truck through the serpentine to get off the compound. post. Almost immediately after we left the wire, I saw old Iraqi fighter jets sitting along the roadway. These jets had been buried by Saddam's air force to avoid their destruction during the invasion. They had recently been dug up. We also drove through several small villages filled with seemingly indifferent civilians without incident. We soon found ourselves at the entrance to ASP Wolf.

ASP Wolf consisted of several partially destroyed buildings surrounded by an earthen berm topped with C-wire. Guard shacks overlooked both the front and rear entrances. The berm was square-shaped with a bunker guarding each corner. The entire compound was maybe three hundred meters wide by four hundred meters long. We spent the next several days shuttling platoons out to ASP Wolf from Al Asad. We then set about fortifying the positions to increase all-around security.

Second Platoon initially stayed at Al Asad, then Haditha Dam, before joining us later in the summer. Our daily schedule consisted of one platoon on guard duty, one platoon on patrol, and one platoon on work detail. We maintained that schedule for the first month. The patrols consisted of clearing our sector of Route Bronze of IEDs. We also conducted security patrols around the scattered ammunition to deter people from stealing the munitions. These patrols were all relatively uneventful, as there were no large population centers in our area of operations (AO).

Shortly after arriving at ASP Wolf, we got an addition to our squad. Each squad was supposed to have three fire teams, but we were short-staffed and only had two. Cpl. Jeremy Laforce was sent to us to help make up for our shortfalls. He was a stout Mexican American from California. He was senior to both Landers and Bowman, so he was given Bowman's team. Bowman went to Landers's team to bolster his numbers.

Cpl. Laforce was an experienced marine. Shortly after meeting him, I could tell he was a level-headed and even-tempered leader. He always treated his subordinates with respect, regardless of their experience level.

During these first few weeks, I also became friendly with another marine, Cpl. Gentian Marku. Marku was a team leader in Second Squad who was born in Albania. He had a thick accent and was sometimes hard to understand. He took a liking to me and often made sure I didn't get shafted when it came to guard rosters and work details. The worst detail to have was burning the waste in the latrines. I usually avoided having to burn barrels of human excrement with diesel fuel due to his kindly intervention.

CHAPTER 7

After being in the country a month, the battalion got tasked with supporting an ongoing operation in Ramadi. Bravo Company took over security for the entire battalion's AO while the other companies supported this Ramadi operation.

Third Platoon was left alone at ASP Wolf for the next four weeks. The other platoons took over patrolling at Haditha Dam and Al Asad. Our patrols became squad-level activities. We would load up 3–4 HMMWVs and drive on Route Bronze and through the ammo-storage area. Our patrols would look for any signs of IEDs but never found anything. We would often see whole families stealing scrap metal and old munitions. These people would be detained and turned over to the Iraqi police.

The Marines had a contract with a local man whose workers broke down the explosive shells by hand using hammers and chisels. Much of our time not spent on patrols consisted of pulling security on these workers. I was always amazed they didn't blow themselves up hammering away on artillery shells with a five-pound hammer. We called this watch detail Jabba Watch, as the rotund man who held the contract reminded us of Jabba the Hutt.

The company reconsolidated in early August, and we were given our first real mission. Intelligence reports indicated that insurgents were hiding weapons caches somewhere along the east bank of the Euphrates. The battalion tasked us with finding and destroying these caches by clearing the suspected area.

We rode to our battalion headquarters in Haditha Dam in the back of LMTVs the day before the operation. Haditha Dam didn't have enough space to house us inside, so we slept that night on the road atop the dam. The night air was warm, and the concrete was still radiating heat as we lay down in full kit to try to sleep. I listened to the waters of Lake Qadisiyah lapping against the side of the dam as I drifted off to sleep.

Cpl. Laforce woke me up at 0300. I looked around and saw the rest of the squad packing up and getting ready to move. I quickly threw my poncho liner into my assault pack and brushed my teeth. I didn't have much time to lose.

Within ten minutes, we loaded up in the backs of the trucks. I looked around at the sleepy faces of my squadmates through my NVGs. I could tell by the worn looks that they had not slept well either. Everyone was sleepily peering through their NVGs, looking into the darkness for any sign of a threat.

The trucks stopped on the northern edge of Barwana, across the river from the city of Haditha. We were now at the southern edge of our search area. We unloaded the trucks and established a 360-degree security perimeter. I leaned against a large palm tree and attempted to adjust my NVGs. Their weight pressing against my forehead was beginning to give me a headache.

The trucks were making a considerable racket between their running engines and the constant hissing of their air brakes. We were waiting on the convoy to move out, but the trucks didn't all have radios. The convoy commander was racing from truck to truck, trying to get a handle on the situation. After about ten minutes, he succeeded in getting everyone herded in the right direction. For the first time, we were plunged into silence. I could hear the sound of the Euphrates flowing off to my left. Occasionally I caught the muffled voices of one of the NCOs adjusting the perimeter.

We were waiting for the sun to rise so we could better search for the weapons caches. We sat there for a half-hour before there was enough light for us to see. As the sun rose, we set off to begin clearing our assigned sectors. Our company's left flank was anchored on the river. Platoons were roughly in line, clearing south to north. We walked for several hours in this manner, methodically searching palm groves, sheds, and any other areas where enemy weapons could have been held. We did not search anyone's homes, as we were not authorized to enter them without due cause.

We soon reached a long pontoon bridge that connected the west bank of the Euphrates to an island in the middle of the river. Another bridge connected the island to the city of Haditha on the river's eastern bank. We stopped so Lt. Wilkens could talk with an older man who was working in a nearby field. Suddenly there was a massive explosion four hundred meters away. Another soon followed it, and then a third.

"Mortars!" Laforce cried out. We all instinctively crouched down. I stared at the dust rising into the blue sky. Laforce's warning snapped me back to reality. I took cover in a nearby ditch as a precaution, although I felt no immediate danger due to the distance. I felt the whole affair was rather anticlimactic from what I had initially expected.

GySgt. Parry came running up to Sgt. Hayden. Parry believed the mortars were coming from across the river. He ordered Third Squad to rush across the narrow bridge and establish security on the far side, which was several hundred meters across the rickety pontoon bridge.

"Let's go, guys," shouted Laforce. Houck, Neely, Laforce, and I raced across the bridge. We quickly made it to the small island and then the east bank of the river. We established far-side security for the rest of the platoon to follow.

A bridge connected the island to a short road, then an intersection. Several locals were walking about the area but quickly dispersed once they saw us.

"Saxby, hop over that wall and see if there's

a way onto that rooftop," Laforce ordered. He pointed toward a five-foot stone wall that surrounded a house overlooking the intersection. Putting someone on the roof would allow us to control the immediate area around the bridge.

I slung my rifle and pulled myself onto the stone wall. Once atop the wall, I could see that the courtyard around the house appeared to be clear. White linen sheets were hanging on a clothesline.

I jumped down into the courtyard and began to make my way toward the house. As I moved through the linen, I heard shouting. I saw movement out of the corner of my eye. I turned toward the movement, just in time to feel a straw broom hit the top of my helmet. What I hadn't seen from my perch on the wall was the old woman hanging clothes on the line. The laundry must have hidden her. My sudden appearance in her backyard scared the daylight out of her. She was now screaming at me and swatting me with her broom.

I quickly backpedaled, trying to calm her down. Within a few moments, an old man emerged from the house to see what the commotion was. I assumed he was the woman's husband. He assessed the situation and grabbed the broom out of the woman's hand. He ushered her into the house. I was utterly taken aback by the entire affair. The last thing I'd expected was to be whacked on the head with a broom by a woman who reminded me of my grandma.

I decided the aggravation wasn't worth any tactical advantage a rooftop position would hold. I quickly retreated over the wall and rejoined my team. I sheepishly looked at the ground as I told Laforce I couldn't get on the roof. He seemed to buy this answer and told me to pull security and wait for the rest of the platoon. I took a position alongside Neely on the south side of the intersection.

As soon as I took up my position, five local men approached me. They looked to be in their early twenties and fit the description of who we would call *military-aged males*. They stopped short of us and began to talk among themselves. They soon began to cautiously walk toward us as if they were trying to gauge our reactions. I could see no weapons, so I stood in their way, blocking their path.

"Turn around," I yelled, gesturing with my hand. The men kept coming, so I yelled again. By now, they had closed the distance and were just outside of arm's length. I held my ground; Neely trained his SAW on them.

A tall, lanky one with jet-black hair appeared to be the leader. He stood directly in front of me. I could tell he was sizing me up with his eyes. I could feel the hatred in his gaze.

"Get the fuck back before I blow your fucking brains all over this goddamned pavement," snarled a voice immediately behind me. The voice was Sgt. Wells's. The men couldn't understand Wells's words, but they understood his tone. The group beat a hasty retreat without further incident.

"Don't let them get within arm's reach again," chided Wells. He then walked away, never mentioning the incident again. We never did find any weapons caches or the source of the three mortar rounds. Soon, we crossed back over the bridge and met the trucks at our designated extraction point.

Our battle rhythm at ASP Wolf went back to usual for the remainder of the summer. In July, the battalion received its first casualty when the scout sniper section was attacked with an IED near Haditha. Several marines were injured, and one was killed. Walker was selected to transfer to the sniper section as a replacement.

The next major operation we conducted was on September 11, 2004, when we recaptured the city of Hīt. Insurgents had taken control of the town and driven out the local police.

The operation in Hīt began on October 12 when we consolidated at the Al Asad Airbase. The scout sniper team from HHC Company was sent in before the main body to reconnoiter enemy positions. They engaged several insurgents as they infiltrated into their objectives. From the information we received at the squad level, it appeared that the insurgents had fled the city ahead of our arrival.

We set up in an attack position outside of Hīt in the predawn hours. Once it was light enough to see, we began to move toward the city. To reach the city, we had to cross a large open field that was the town's dump. Judging from the awful smell and the piles of refuse I observed as we crossed it, I would say the folks in military intelligence finally got something right.

We received no opposition as we moved into the city. We quickly occupied the local soccer stadium and used that as the company command post. The company commander ordered our platoon to clear the local police station. I was detailed to help provide outer security, but the rest of the team went inside. The insurgents had run off the local police and raised a hand-sewn Iraqi flag on the pole. The battalion Intel section told us the group was Ba'ath Party sympathizers. This explained the flag. Houck took the flag down from the pole and later traded it to me for a case of soda from the PX.

We patrolled through Hīt rather uneventfully for the remainder of the day. We encountered several groups of bearded Americans whom I speculated were Army Special Forces. They had limited interactions with my platoon, though. We pulled out of the city in the early evening. We returned first to Al Asad, then back to ASP Wolf.

The missions in Haditha and Hīt were the only non-routine operations we took part in between July and October 2004. By the end of the summer, most of us boots had been promoted from PFC to LCpl. We kept hearing rumors that a massive operation was being planned to retake the insurgent stronghold of Fallujah, but they were only rumors.

CHAPTER 8

One hot, sunny day in early October, we got the news we had all been waiting on. We were conducting a live-fire weapons range at ASP Wolf. Our ACOG sights on our M16A4s had to be readjusted every so often to keep their site alignment. We called this maintaining their dope. We tried to do it every month if the ammunition allowed.

Lt. Wilkens had set up silhouette targets at distances of twenty-five to one hundred meters on the west side of the FOB. He had us tape boxes of strawberry milk from the chow hall in various places on the targets. He said it was to simulate blood when we scored hits, but I suspected it was to eliminate the growing supply we had. The stuff was so disgusting that nobody would drink it, yet we got more of it in every resupply.

We were plugging away on the makeshift range when Sgt. Hayden approached the firing line. He told the team he needed to talk to everyone once we had cleared the range.

"There's going to be another big push into Fallujah," he told us as we huddled around him. "We've been tapped to support it in some capacity. Expect to move out of here later this month." He confided he didn't know much more than that. He had just received the warning order from Lt.

Wilkens.

We were released to help clean up the range. The rest of the day, we talked about how awesome it would be to leave the tedious daily grind at ASP Wolf. We all longed for some real action. Later that evening, Rodriguez, Lambotte, and I talked about everything we would buy when we got to Camp Fallujah PX. At this point, we had been pretty much isolated from any real American consumer goods for over four months. The occasional PX truck would infrequently arrive at the FOB, but this only whetted our appetite for more.

We began to talk about all the various cereals we hadn't had, leading to nostalgic talks about foods we missed back home. Later that night, I decided to write to my mom and ask her to mail me boxes of different sugary cereals. I implored her that the "fate of the free world" depended on it.

A few days after receiving the warning order, Lt. Wilkens taught us a series of classes. First, we learned a brief history of Fallujah's part in the ongoing insurgency in the country. In April 2004, the US had unsuccessfully tried to wrest control of the city back from the Sunni insurgents who had taken power after the invasion. The catalyst for Operation Vigilant Resolve, or the First Battle of Fallujah, had been the murder of four US contractors in March. The men had been ambushed and killed in downtown Fallujah. Insurgents had hung their bodies from a bridge over the Euphrates.

The American commanders had called off the attack after political pressure from Iraqi authorities over the amount of damage to the city. The Sunni insurgency had declared a victory as US forces had withdrawn from the city. Over the next several months, the insurgents had worked to consolidate their positions and fortify their defenses.

Lt. Wilkens then spoke with us about the Russian experiences in Chechnya in the 1990s. The Russians had entered that city with a robust mechanized presence, which had been unsupported by infantry. He further described how the Russian convoy had been cut to pieces by anti-armor weapons fired from short ranges in the tanks' blind spots.

The lessons from Chechnya about the importance of combined arms tactics helped us understand the importance of cooperation. The infantry would clear the complex terrain the tanks couldn't, and in return, the armored tanks would provide direct fire support to reduce enemy strongholds. This close cooperation would be vitally important in the weeks to come.

We also ran through a bayonet assault course. The course was a series of old tires on the perimeter of the FOB. The bayonet training served as both PT and to instill an aggressive spirit in us. Racing through the course at a full sprint, screaming, and plunging the eight inches of steel of the OKC-3S bayonet into the pliable rubber was therapeutic. I imagined the rubber and wood targets as living, breathing human beings trying to kill me. It helped keep me focused.

We departed ASP Wolf on October 31. The hot desert nights had started to become cold. We were replaced by a company of reservists who were taking control of the entire Haditha AO. They arrived in a single long convoy of five-ton trucks. These same trucks would take us first to Al Asad, then on to Camp Fallujah the next night.

Some of the marines had started a small bonfire with scraps of wood while we waited to load the trucks. This small fire soon saw the addition of several tires from the bayonet assault course. By the time we loaded the trucks to leave, a bonfire had lit the night air. There was almost a carnival atmosphere as we left the sheltered safety of ASP Wolf, never to return.

The drive from ASP Wolf to Al Asad Airbase in the back of the five-tons was relatively uneventful. We had done the trip many times before. We stayed the next day in the tents at Al Asad. They wanted us to move only at night to keep the convoys safer and disguise how many troops were massing for the upcoming battle. On the night of November 1, we convoyed to Camp Fallujah. The night air was freezing in the uncovered vehicles.

We huddled together and tried to stay warm. I sat next to Houck in the front of the truck bed. He and I took turns alternating between sleeping and staying on watch. We couldn't see much in the darkness, and most of us didn't bother putting on our NVGs. We arrived at Camp Fallujah just as the sun was beginning to rise.

Camp Fallujah had initially been built by Saddam Hussein to train the Mujahedin-e-Khalq, or the People's Mujahedin of Iran, an Iranian dissident group supported by Iraq during the Iran-Iraq War. The buildings we stayed in were open bays lined with space for army cots. There was no glass in the windows or electricity. Kerosene heaters heated the bays. It appeared as if nobody had occupied this section of the compound in some time.

Upon arrival, each platoon was assigned to a squad bay. We weren't able to get the cots issued until later in the day, so most of us slept on our sleeping mats on the concrete porch surrounding the bays. The morning air was cold, but most of us were so tired we barely noticed.

I had been asleep for only an hour when a large explosion awakened me. It was the sound of an incoming rocket hitting the perimeter approximately four hundred meters away. The sound of outgoing artillery quickly followed the noise of the impact. Radar systems that could detect incoming rounds ringed the base. This network triangulated a point of origin (POO). A battery of 155 mm howitzers assigned a counterfire mission then targeted the POO. These indirect fire exchanges became a daily, if not hourly, occurrence during our time in Camp Fallujah. We quickly grew accustomed to the explosions and learned to ignore them.

We spent the rest of that first day resting and unpacking our gear. We were told to separate our equipment between what we would need in the city and what remained behind. The commander gave us a strict packing list to adhere to for the upcoming battle. We also got the opportunity to go to the main PX on base and use the phone and internet lounge.

I bought myself a large black assault pack, which I planned on using for the upcoming operation. I then went to the internet café and called my parents. I used one of the computers to email a girl back home named Michelle, who had been sending me care packages throughout my deployment.

The next day we began planning and rehearsing in earnest. Lt. Wilkens issued us a platoon-level operations order, which outlined our objectives for the first days of the assault. Third Platoon was being augmented with several attachments for the mission. We would have machine-gun teams from the weapons platoon, a mortar team with a 60 mm mortar, a S.M.A.W. team, and a squad of engineers trained in demolition operations.

Lt. Wilkens described how the first phase of the operation was supposed to play out. We would depart Camp Fallujah in AAVs. AAV is the name given to the AAV-P7, a type of amphibious troop transport used by the marines in Iraq. This movement would take place before the sun rose. We would move to an assault position north of the city, where we would remain throughout the day. Once it became dark, we would continue to the railroad tracks, which lay immediately outside the northern edge of the city limits. We would hold here until the engineers could create a breach lane in the Mujahedin minefield protecting the city. We would then dismount, cross the breach, and move south toward our first objective.

During the first phase of the assault, the battalion's objective was to seize the government compound in the city's northern end. There were three company-level sub-objectives that had to be taken. Bravo Company and Charlie would seize the Islamic Cultural Center and would take the Al Hadrah Mosque. Alpha Company would then pass through our lines and seize the mayor's complex immediately south of Bravo and Charlie. Once the battalion had secured the initial objectives, Lt. Wilkens told us we would then have follow-on missions to secure the rest of the city. We would selectively clear key terrain to seize the city, then turn around and systematically clear every building.

After the platoon operations order, we began our rehearsals. The company had to work closely with marine tank forces during the operation. We had extraordinarily little training in working with tracked vehicles, though. Army M113s would provide our medical evacuation support. Marine Corps M1A1s would provide tank support, and assault amphibious vehicles (AAV-7A1s) would give a mounted platform for our dismounted infantry. The tanks and AAVs would also provide close infantry support in the complex terrain of the city.

Our first introduction to these vehicles was a "petting zoo," in which operators parked the vehicles outside our living area and allowed us to crawl all over the vehicles. The operators gave us a capability brief and answered any questions the marines had about the vehicles. The medics taught us how to load casualties into the M113s properly.

The medics operating the M113s were all Army National Guardsmen. The period of instruction was taught by one of their NCOs. As he spoke to us, I could not help but notice what appeared to be dried blood staining his boots. The brownish rust color contrasted with the dusty tan of the suede boot. I tried to remain focused on the class instead of imagining what it would be like to bleed out all over the back of the cramped and dark vehicle.

We also conducted practice patrols with the tanks and AAVs every chance we got between the fourth and seventh of November. When the vehicles were not available, we conducted dismounted patrols among the buildings of Camp Fallujah. The sporadic incoming rocket and mortar fire added a sense of realism and urgency to our training.

On the seventh of November, we conducted our final rehearsals. The final exercise was a dress rehearsal of the mounted convoy to our assault positions. We loaded into the noisy AAVs and rode around Camp Fallujah. We ended up at the gate, where we practiced dismounting before returning to the billeting area.

After the rehearsal, we were given the rest of the day off. All our bags were packed, staged, and ready to move. We consolidated any equipment we weren't taking with us in duffel bags stored in the company headquarters area. The first sergeant chose a detail from each platoon to remain behind and guard the baggage. LCpl. Fonda was selected from Third Platoon. Houck had also been nominated to go to battalion headquarters for the first phase of the battle, as he was qualified to operate the Dragon Eye Unmanned Aerial Vehicle (UAV). Our squad was down two marines for the initial push. Both men would rejoin us later in the battle.

We also had a *New York Times* reporter and photographer traveling with our platoon into the city. The reporter's name was Dexter Filkins, and the photographer was Ashley Gilbertson. We were suspicious of them because they weren't prior military. We believed they would do something stupid to get someone killed, so we viewed their presence more as a liability than as a benefit.

We spent the rest of the day trying not to focus on the upcoming battle. Nobody talked about it at first. Many of the marines in the platoon passed the time playing baseball outside the barracks. The game quickly became a focal point for the company. The game served as a temporary distraction to the gnawing uncertainty we all faced.

I was not one for sports. Instead, I spent the afternoon reading a book about the Vietnam War. Later, I engaged in a spirited debate with Rodriquez, Holmes, and Parker on the Iraq War's merits. We all had varying opinions on what exactly we were doing there—not that our convictions mattered at that point. We would be heading into the cauldron in the morning, whether we agreed with the reasons or not.

When darkness fell, we all lay on our cots and pretended to sleep. Not many of us got a full night's sleep; the uneasiness for what was to come kept most of us awake. At 0300, the wait was over. GySgt. Parry came into the platoon bay and roused us all from our beds. It was time to earn our pay.

CHAPTER 9

We donned all our equipment and formed up on the road. The weight of the AT4 dug into my shoulder, causing me to shift my weight as GySgt. Parry got his headcount. We were all overloaded. Every marine carried his full combat load of eight thirty-round magazines, IBA, weapon, and Kevlar helmet. Each squad had a breaching kit spread among its members. I was assigned to carry the maul. I kept thinking how insane it was that it was 2004, and I was taking an ax into battle. We also had sandbags, water, and rations. Every marine was given either an AT4, a S.M.A.W. rocket, or a 60 mm mortar round.

GySgt. Parry marched us through the buildings of Camp Fallujah to our assembly area. As we walked, I quickly worked up a sweat from the heavy weight of the equipment. I was glad we were riding to the city on the AAVs and could not wait to share some of the massive amounts of ammo I was carrying with the enemy.

We loaded onto the waiting AAVs in the assembly area. As the heavy armored door raised, we were plunged into darkness. I felt as if that heavily armored door had closed on my coffin. All of Third Squad was crammed into the same vehicle. I watched the sunrise that morning through the vision periscope in the back of the AAV while we waited to convoy out of Camp Fallujah.

As the convoy left, I sat in the back of the vehicle with my eyes closed. I tried to sleep, but a combination of nerves and the jostling of the AAV over the uneasy terrain kept sleep at bay. The back of the vehicle was dark; once the sun rose, there was a sliver of light through the rear vision port. This shaft of light cast a dark shadow on everyone.

We had just gotten out of Camp Fallujah when our vehicle broke down. The engine just stopped running. We sat there in the back of the vehicle, completely helpless. The crew desperately tried to breathe life back into their stricken vehicle. Finally, they got the engine running again. We continued toward our attack position.

We arrived in the attack position early in the morning. It was a patch of barren, rocky desert roughly two kilometers north of the city. It overlooked the rail line, which ran just outside the city's perimeter. Between the railroad tracks and the city's streets was the suspected enemy minefield we were to breach.

Once we dismounted in the attack position, we quickly began to establish security. We would be in these positions until after sunset. We were within the enemy's indirect fire range, so we started to dig in. The ground was as hard as concrete. Neely and I partnered up to dig a hasty fighting position. After working on it for the better part of four hours, we had scraped only a shallow six-inch grave into the dirt. We eventually gave up, and whenever the battalion's line received a sporadic mortar round, we crowded into this hole. Fortunately, nothing came even remotely close to hitting us.

Fixed-wing aircraft flew overhead, strafing and bombing enemy positions while rotary-wing aircraft hovered outside the city limits, engaging targets. The helicopter pilots would not pass over the city for fear of getting shot down by rocket-propelled grenades (RPGs).

Neely and I lay together in our little hole and wondered if any resistance was left after the awesome firepower display we'd witnessed. I figured it would be like Hīt, all hyped up but with an enemy who would not stay and fight. Neely thought that they would stay and fight. We decided we would figure it out shortly enough.

As the sun began to set, we got the order to mount back up in our AAVs. We quickly loaded into ours, but the crew couldn't get it started. GySgt. Parry made the call to split Third Squad up among the other AAVs in the company. Neely, the two reporters, and I ended up crammed in an AAV with the company headquarters section. It was already fully loaded before we got to it, and the addition of four more made it impossible to move.

We were packed in like sardines in a can, my body pressed against the rear door. There was a speaker box off to my right, which was set to the company frequency. I could hear Capt. Omohundro getting the platoons into position as the engineers prepared to breach the minefield.

Suddenly I heard what sounded like hail hitting the outside of the vehicle, pinging off the other side of the door that I was crammed against. I listened to the vehicle commander let loose with his machine gun. It was then that I accepted what I already knew deep inside. It wasn't hail hitting the vehicle; it was enemy bullets.

"Suppress that rooftop; they got a machine gun!" an unknown voice squawked from the radio speaker. The vehicle commander's machine gun barked a response. I sat pressed against the heavy door, powerless to move as I listened to the bullets impacting against it.

My mind raced to a movie I had seen years before depicting the D-Day landings. The movie's soldiers had been crammed into a Higgins boat, just as we were crammed into these AAVs. When the doors to the Higgins boat had dropped, the men inside had been cut to pieces by the German machine guns. The men in the movie had been powerless to save themselves. I sat and listened to the pinging of the bullets and wondered if I would share their fates.

Suddenly, the pinging halted. The AAV's M240 kept firing, but the enemy fire had stopped. They must have suppressed the enemy position. I didn't have much time to think about it before I heard the firing commands for the Mine-Clearing Line Charge (MCLC), which would breach the enemy minefield.

The MCLC was an explosive "rope" fired from a vehicle. The charge's explosion cleared a lane eight meters by one hundred meters. I heard the engineer squad over the radio giving their preparatory firing commands.

The MCLC failed to explode; a young sapper had to rush out and manually detonate it. After the explosion, I heard the metallic sound of the ramp unlocking, then felt the door begin to fall. The weight of the men and equipment behind me caused me to fall onto the ramp. Everyone behind me was rushing off, forcing me to crawl on my hands and knees onto the rocky soil. The weight of my equipment slammed against my back as I rolled onto the ground.

The sky was pitch black. The only light was from several small fires set by the MCLC and the mines. These fires cast shadows across everything as they slowly burned out. I was up against a small berm with train tracks on top. Neely was kneeling right beside me.

"Have you seen Cpl. Laforce or Sgt. Hayden?" I asked him.

"No, have you?" he replied.

I looked around and then searched through the lenses of my NVGs. I saw the two reporters. I asked them if they had seen anyone from our platoon. They hadn't either. I was starting to get nervous as the marines around me began racing toward the breach lane on the far side of the berm. Neely and

I figured we would probably be able to find someone on the far side of the breach, so we followed the mass of men streaming into the city.

The *breach lane* was considered the area cleared by the line charge. The breach master had marked the lane with glowing chem lights and white engineer tape. A marine on the near side guided everyone through. As we began to race through the breach, I heard a loudspeaker on a nearby HMMWV blasting the rock song "Hells Bells." It was a psyops unit attempting to use the music to scare the enemy. I thought the music paired well with the sounds of shouting men, diesel engines, and gunfire.

As we neared the far side of the breach lane, I saw GySgt. Parry. He was standing at the far side, directing marines toward their respective squads and platoons. "Third's over there," he gruffly directed before yelling at another wayward soul. Neely and I quickly rejoined our platoon and found Cpl. Laforce.

Once we had everyone accounted for, we slowly began to make our way into the city streets. The suppressive gunfire from the vehicles at the breach site could still be heard in the distance. The city still had electricity, and the mosques were blaring jihadi music and slogans from the minaret loudspeakers. The psyops trucks countered it with a mixture of heavy rock metal, sonar pings, and whale calls. Once we cleared the edge of the city, the distant sound of gunfire began to slacken. It appeared that the defenders had fled deeper into the city.

The platoon patrolled together in a tactical column. First Squad under Sgt. Wells led the way; folllowed by Second. Third Squad was in the rear. We cleared a courtyard and a house as soon as we got inside the city. Lt. Wilkens gained radio contact with the company commander and got his bearings on the map. We hadn't received any opposition since clearing the breach point. I saw no sign of any civilians still remaining in the city.

After a short halt in the courtyard, we continued moving farther south into the city. Just before midnight, the power to the city was finally cut. I didn't know if the US military cut the power or if the effects of the fighting did. The loss of power silenced the calls to arms blasting from the minarets. Our interpreter, Ajax, told us the loudspeakers were playing music glorifying martyrdom and giving US troops' locations. Ajax was a Jamaican who had been studying Arabic in Baghdad before the invasion. He had stayed in Iraq to work with US forces.

We continued to make our way south for another block. We entered another courtyard to do another map check. It was here that Lt. Wilkens realized he had lost his map. He hadn't noticed that his pocket had ripped while climbing over a wall. The map had fallen out of his pocket at some point since the previous short halt. Sgt. Wells volunteered to go back with him to look for it, as he, too, had lost something. He said he'd had a ziplock bag with his poker winnings and his wedding ring in his cargo pocket, and he thought it had fallen out during the halt.

Our fire team was assigned to accompany Lt. Wilkens and Sgt. Wells back to the courtyard. We left the platoon in position and quickly made our way back through the abandoned streets. I could hear heavy automatic weapons fire in the distance. Occasionally, tracers and flares would arc into the air.

As we made our way back, I began to wonder how strange it was to be in an almost abandoned city. The coalition authorities had launched an extensive and relatively successful public-information campaign in the months leading up to the battle. This campaign had warned residents to evacuate the city ahead of the upcoming offensive. It had also given them safe passage to outlying areas. Almost the entire population had heeded the warning. Most of those who remained behind were there to fight.

We soon found ourselves at the edge of the city. We stepped into the clearing where the city met the desert and was immediately greeted with the sound of a .50-caliber machine gun firing. The gun was firing at a target only one hundred meters west of our location. Sgt. Wells immediately suggested we get moving. After several minutes we finally made our way to the courtyard. Wells and Wilkens searched for their items while we pulled security. Wilkens found his map, but I never learned if Wells found his wedding band. We searched for several minutes before heading back towards the platoon.

We quickly rejoined the platoon in the courtyard we had left them in. We had to remain in a defensive position to allow adjacent units to get into position for the advance. Both Bravo Company and Charlie Company were moving up in a line to avoid gaps that could be exploited by small Mujahedin squads.

Third Squad was on the rooftop, providing security. I was downstairs sitting on the couch. Cpl. Laforce and Neely were seated next to me. Sgt. Wells was sitting in a recliner across the room from me. Other members of the First and Second Squads rested wherever they could fit in the room. We were all exhausted from the day's activities.

Platoon 3073, Lima Company, 3rd Recruit Training Battalion graduated on September 19, 2003 from Parris Island. This is the first family visit that recruits get in 13 weeks!

The author takes a break during training at SOI, October 2003. Training during the School of Infantry helped prepare young Marines for the rigors of Iraq.

B Team, 2nd Squad, 3rd Platoon during the Second Battle of Fallujah. Left to Right: Alexander Saxby, Charles Neely, Jeremy Laforce and David Houck. Photo courtesy of Robbie Landers.

3rd Platoon, Bravo Company, 1st Battalion, 8th Marines, Regimental Combat Team 7, July 2004 at ASP Wolf, Al Anbar, Iraq.

The view from the top of Haditha Dam, Summer 2004. The dam was used by the battalion as a headquarters. Photo courtesy of Daniel Bystricky.

Third Platoon rests during the operation in Hit, October 2004. Left to Right: Daniel Osborn, David Houck, Alexander Saxby, Michael Gordon, Jeremy Laforce. Photo courtesy of Robbie Landers.

Left to Right: Michael Rodriguez, Joel Lambotte, Alexander Saxby. Photo taken at ASP Wolf in October, 2004 immediatly after the operation in Hit, Iraq.

David Houck sitting on a rooftop in Hit after the Battalion recaptured the city, October 2004. Photo courtesy of Robbie Landers.

Bystricky posing for the camera on the M2 .50 cal Machine Gun at the enterence to ASP Wolf, Summer 2004. Photo courtesy of Daniel Bystricky.

2nd Squad, 3rd Platoon standing outside the barracks at ASP Wolf, summer 2004.

Alexander Saxby sits with Doc Lambotte on November 8th 2004 in the company assault position, north of Fallujah. Photo courtesy of Robbie Landers.

Marines prepare weapons in the assault position just north of Fallujah. The AAVs can be seen in the background. Photo courtesy of Daniel Bystricky.

Charles Neely (foreground) and the Saxby (standing) dig in at the assault position prior to the attack, 8 November 2004. Photo courtesy of Robbie Landers.

Smoke rises from an airstrike during the fighting in Fallujah, November 2004. Photo courtesy of Daniel Bystricky.

Daniel Bystricky manning an M240 Machine Gun on a convoy prior to the battle. Photo courtesy of Daniel Bystricky.

Lcpl Saxby recieves the Navy and Marine Corps Achievement Medal with V Device for dragging Crist to the casualty collection point on the first day of the fighting. September, 2005.

David Houck following his graduation from recruit training at Parris Island, SC on June 6, 2002. David wanted to be a career Marine. Photo courtesy of Beth Houck.

David Houck is buried in Section 60 of Arlington National Cemetary. He is buried nearby several other fallen members of the 1st Battalion 8th Marines.

CHAPTER 10

I must have drifted off, because I awoke to the sound of gunfire. I quickly surmised from all the shouting that Third Squad was currently engaged in a firefight on the rooftop. Not wanting to miss out on the action, I raced upstairs. Cpl. Straub, one of the Third Squad team leaders, was trying to direct everyone's fire onto the target. I couldn't understand what he was trying to get us to fire at, but I was ready for action.

I ran toward the low wall and found an open spot to occupy. I still couldn't see what everyone was shooting at. I picked a rooftop in Straub's target area's general vicinity and began to suppress it with fire. Lambotte was standing next to me, his M9 pistol in his hand. He fired a round.

I turned to him and asked, "What are we shooting at?"

"I have no fucking idea," he replied.

By now, GySgt. Parry had made his way to the rooftop. He was demanding to know what our target was. He screamed at everyone to cease firing. The shooting stopped. Straub explained that a man with a gun was in the street and had ducked into a building. We were currently shooting at this building. GySgt. Parry told us to remain vigilant but not waste our ammo unless we had a definitive target.

I was excited now. Although it wasn't much of anything, I finally got the chance to shoot my weapon. *"This whole war thing isn't that bad after all,"* I thought to myself.

Within an hour, the sun began to rise on the morning of November 9, 2004. We got the order to continue moving south just as the sun was starting to rise. By this point, we were about five blocks north of our objective, the Islamic Cultural Center. First Platoon was to our right, and Second was to their right. To our left was Phase Line Ethan and Charlie Company beyond.

As we moved south, First Squad reported movement to our immediate left. We took cover in a courtyard and cleared the house within. I found myself on the rooftop with First Squad. Cpl. Silva, a team leader from First, directed our attention to the rooftops to our east. I could see people moving around and tried to identify them through my ACOG sight. I couldn't get a positive identification on them. Other marines were also trying to identify them. A nearby marine asked Silva if we should fire.

"Hold up," he said. "The sniper team's coming up, and they should be able to get better eyes on."

As he said that, the team leader for the attached sniper team stepped out onto the roof with us. Cpl. Dominic Esquibel was a thin man with a severe look on his face. He wore the issued "birth control" glasses on his face. We called the issued glasses birth control because they were so ugly that the wearer would never be able to find a sexual partner, so they served as a form of birth control. He peered through his scope at the people moving on the rooftops.

"I think they're marines," he said.

Silva informed Lt. Wilkens, and we began moving again. We hadn't gone more than one hundred feet when I heard an Abrams tank moving toward us. Just as the tank reached our position, I heard a loud swooshing sound followed by an explosion in the air. The already eerie gray dawn was quickly filled with smoke and fire. The small fireballs fell all around us, consuming anything they touched. Thick, acrid smoke filled the air.

Somehow nobody had been hit by the fireballs. I initially thought the tank had fired its smoke canisters, but there was too much fire and smoke for this to be the case. We quickened our pace to get out of the area. I later learned that we had been near a white phosphorous (WP) shell that had exploded above

us. The gunner's target had been an enemy squad that had worked its way between us and Charlie Company. I don't know how nobody was injured.

We continued to clear the area of the WP round. Radio chatter from battalion told us that the battalion scout snipers had taken casualties in the vicinity of Regimental Objective One, the regiment's name for the Islamic Cultural Center. A heavy burst of gunfire erupted from the area of First Platoon's position. The company radio net filled with contact reports.

First Platoon had engaged a vehicle and killed several enemy fighters. One of them had detonated a suicide vest as the marines had gotten closer. No marines had been injured during the engagement, but four insurgents had been killed.

First and Second Platoons were establishing overwatch positions on the cultural center. They would serve as support by fire for our platoon to occupy the building and relieve the SEAL and recon teams already inside. The casualty from the scout sniper section was located with First Platoon.

We continued pushing on. We quickly linked up with a squad from First Platoon who was providing overwatch down an alleyway. The rest of the platoon was helping to medevac the sniper section's casualty. Lying in the middle of the street was the first human corpse I had ever seen. The man looked to be in his early twenties with short, curly black hair and a jet-black beard. His head had been split open by a bullet, and he was lying on his back. His brain was half out of his skull and displayed on the pavement in a puddle of blood. His skin had a waxy appearance.

He wore a dark-gray shirt and matching sweatpants. He had a black chest rig filled with AK-47 magazines over his slightly plump body. His rifle lay on the street beside him, where it had fallen.

His fingers were extended, reaching out toward the buttstock as if he was trying to grasp it.

Nearby was a gold Jeep Cherokee. All four doors were open. The driver was dead behind the wheel. Bullet holes riddled the SUV. Another dead man lay beside the passenger-side door. Inside was another rifle and an RPG.

Doc Lambotte ran up to me as we passed the macabre scene. "Dude, Walker got hit," he told me. "He got shot when the sniper section tried crossing a street up ahead. Got shot in the arm, it sounds like." I saw the rest of First Platoon pulling security up ahead.

We halted briefly at First Platoon's location. I didn't know that Walker had already been evacuated, so I went inside to try to find him. While I was inside, my platoon got orders to move out and secure Regimental Objective One.

Second Platoon was providing overwatch about a block west of our current location. The company had a platoon of tanks in support, but I didn't know exactly where those tanks were currently located. The platoon crossed the four-lane highway adjacent to the cultural center and the Al-Hadrah Mosque. It took about five minutes for the entire platoon to cross the street. The company commander and the FiST crossed with us.

In those five minutes and over those four lanes of roadway, we took five casualties. Sgt. Wells was struck in the leg by machine-gun fire. Doc Lambotte and GySgt. Ryan Shane rushed out to save him. Shane ran from Second Platoon's overwatch position and was shot trying to drag Wells to safety. Doc Lambotte was attempting to assist Shane when he was shot in the leg. Sgt. Ken Hudson, a member of the FiST, was shot in his hand, and LCpl. Sam Crist was shot in the groin and arm. Crist was the marine I dragged to the casualty-collection point. With Walker's wound added to the count, that intersection cost First Battalion Eight Marines five WIA and one KIA. A member of the recon platoon was also wounded in the cultural center during the night.

After Capt. Omohundro's decision to call in a danger-close artillery strike, enemy resistance in the mosque abated. Charlie Company was able to move in and secure their objective alongside Iraqi Army personnel. We were able to get ammunition and food resupplied later that morning. By noon, our hold on the area was complete. Conditions were set for Alpha Company to pass through our positions and secure the Mayor's Complex. They accomplished this later in the afternoon.

Later that day, once the fighting had died down a little, we were able to begin to digest what had occurred that day. Lt. Wilkens brought the entire platoon together inside the cultural center and informed us that Sgt. Wells had died. The news hit us all extremely hard, but the information especially tore up his squad. We had all hoped that his wounds were not as serious as they had appeared, that somehow, he would make it.

We spent the night of November 9 at the cultural center. Once the battalion had secured its objectives, Houck was released back to us. We had to wait on the adjacent battalions to secure their objectives before beginning to push south again. Bravo Company maintained platoons in line as we continued to make our way south. T

Third Platoon remained on the left flank of Bravo's line. The platoons selectively cleared their way south. We didn't clear every building —only the ones with a clear strategic value or known enemy strongholds. Once we occupied a building, we would immediately establish overwatch positions on the rooftops. Our snipers would get into a position where they could put accurate fires on the enemy while waiting for the rest of the company to continue the movement.

Snipers were a highly effective weapon in Fallujah. Both sides used them to disrupt enemy formations and clear the streets. The enemy snipers would kill us as we moved into intersections or open areas. One sniper could effectively hold up the entire company's movement for hours.

The tenth of November was a relatively quiet day for Third Platoon. We advanced several blocks south without coming into any significant enemy resistance. Second Platoon was not so lucky, though. Cpl. Romulo Jimenez II was killed by a sniper while crossing a street as the platoon moved in to clear one of the many mosques dotting the city. His loss hit the platoon hard, as they were still reeling from Gunnery Shane's serious injury the day prior.

By nightfall, we were waiting in yet another house and courtyard for the order to continue south. The commander ordered us to move approximately two hundred meters to our east to occupy a sizeable three-story apartment complex for the night. The rest of the company would occupy buildings in the vicinity.

We had to cross a large field to get to the building. Lt. Wilkens decided to use AAVs to shield our movements. They would cross the field while we hid behind them. He radioed for a section of AAVs to escort us across the open field. A team of Abrams tanks provided overwatch for the movement. We huddled behind the armored vehicles and began to move across.

In the darkness, Maxey fell into a hole and twisted his ankle. I was immediately behind him when he fell. I heard him scream and saw him drop. Thinking he had been shot, I reached out to help him. Landers got to him first and brought him to his feet. He could not keep up with our movements, so we put him in the back of the AAV and kept moving to the apartment building.

It took almost an hour to clear the apartment complex. The first floor was a parking area with one central stairwell serving the upstairs apartments. Above the parking area were two floors, each with a long hallway that apartments opened into. The entire building was deserted, and the former occupants had left every door locked. Breaking each lock to clear the area of enemy fighters was exhausting work.

We had to use the breaching kits to open the doors. I used my maul to open two doors before switching off with Laforce. Once we had the entire place cleared, we established a watch rotation to get some rest. Two marines would pull security on the single entrance, while Lt. Wilkens and GySgt. Parry would take turns overseeing everything. An infrared (IR) strobe was placed on the rooftop to mark our position to friendly aircraft overhead.

We had been settled in for only about a half-hour when the first shells came in. I heard a sound like a screaming freight car followed by a massive explosion. The explosion shook the ground, almost as if the earth was gelatin. The round had landed in the street in front of the apartment building.

GySgt. Parry began to yell, asking if everyone was all right, when a second round came in. This one hit behind the building.

"We're bracketed," I heard Lt. Wilkens say. *Bracketing* meant that the enemy mortar crew had found the correct range, and the next round should be a hit. The enemy mortarmen did not disappoint. The third round from the Al Jaleel 82 mm mortar landed right on top of our building.

I sat in the corner of one of the rooms on the third floor. I curled helplessly into the fetal position as the concrete building shook with each mortar impact. I watched helplessly as a crack began to appear in the concrete above me. It grew with each successive round. The shock waves from each impact seemed to lift the building off its foundation before sending dust flying. I was terrified, positive the building was going to fall around me as I watched the walls shake.

"They must have a spotter using the strobe light as a reference point," Fitchett shouted to Lt. Wilkens.

"I'll get it," was all Wilkens replied.

Lt. Wilkens waited for a round to impact, then raced onto the rooftop to retrieve the strobe. The effect of shutting it off was instantaneous. The rounds stopped coming in. Within minutes, the enemy directed their fire to another platoon. It ended when everyone shut off their strobes and observed light discipline. The apartment building had sustained five direct hits, yet we had received no casualties. The entire incident had lasted maybe three minutes, but the screaming shells had turned the minutes to hours.

After we had settled ourselves, we tried to get back to sleep, keeping our two-man watch on the front entrance. Neely woke me up at 0400 so I could stand my watch with Laforce. When we relived Houck, he told us he and Neely had heard movement and talking out in the streets several minutes before. He said that when they'd looked outside, the source of the voices had been gone.

They were both adamant that the voices had not been speaking English.

Laforce and I spent the next hour vigilantly guarding the top of the stairwell. We saw no sign of the source of the noises that Houck had reported. The only noises we heard were the numerous stray dogs prowling about and occasional bursts of gunfire off in the distance. Occasionally a flare would light up the night sky. Both sides were using flares to try and see through the dark streets. After we were relieved, I fell back asleep for another thirty minutes. The stress of the day had left me emotionally and physically spent.

CHAPTER 11

I awoke on the morning of November 11 to GySgt. Parry's cheerful voice screaming at us to get up. He yelled out, "Wake the fuck up! It's Veterans Day, and I guess you all qualify as vets now." He then proceeded to tell Sgt. Hayden that he needed a detail.

Cpl. Esquibel had forgotten a radio in one of the adjacent buildings, and a squad was needed to accompany him to retrieve it. Third Squad was going to be the lucky squad.

"I'm sorry, guys," he sheepishly said to us. "I'll buy you all a steak dinner when we get home."

We set out to retrieve the radio from the hide site his team had been using. A section of AAV's was in contact with the enemy near the buildings. We tried to avoid getting involved in that firefight so we could complete our mission. We quickly reached our objective and secured the wayward radio. We then headed back toward the apartment complex.

As we neared one of the AAVs, I began to hear the crackling of fire. Thick black smoke was coming from an alleyway. We turned the corner, and one of our vehicles was burning. The other marines from the AAV platoon were already evacuating the wounded men. There was little we could do.

Sgt. Hayden led us back to the relative safety of the apartment building.

We stayed in the building for the next few hours as the battalion readjusted its lines. We got the order to move south just before noon. Third Platoon maintained its position in the company formation. Our next stop was in a building about a block south of the apartment. The company commander had authorized the use of a five-hundred-pound bomb against an enemy position, and we had to take cover. We quickly cleared a nearby house and waited for the explosion.

When it came, it rattled every window in the house. I had no idea how far away the detonation was, but it reminded me of the previous night's mortar barrage. We began our move south again shortly after the explosion. We hadn't gone far when we linked up with First Platoon. The company commander had received a new mission, and Lt. Wilkens needed to be briefed.

Capt. Omohundro, 1st Sgt. Whittington, and the platoon commanders were all huddled around a map in the living room. The building was rather large, so we helped with security. First Platoon was engaging enemy positions from the rooftop, so Cpl. Laforce led us out there to help. Cpl. Pennock also led First Squad out to help.

The rooftop was a typical roof with a flat surface surrounded by a waist-high wall. First Platoon had knocked small holes in this wall to serve as firing ports, allowing us to engage targets without exposing ourselves over the ledge. Enemy fighters were engaging from the surrounding buildings with AK-47s.

A platoon of tanks was on the streets surrounding our position, and they were helping to destroy targets. I climbed up next to Pennock and began engaging an enemy position on a balcony approximately three hundred meters away. After emptying a magazine into the balcony, the forward air controller got approval to drop another five-hundred-pound bomb.

We clambered inside to take cover from the explosion. The colossal blast wave rattled the glass as it passed over the building. After the blast, I went downstairs to rest. There I saw LCpl. Holmes getting gauze put around his neck by our new corpsman, Doc Masino. Masino was a replacement for Lambotte after the fight at the Cultural Center. Holmes had been slightly wounded from a piece of shrapnel, but he was refusing evacuation. "It's just a scratch," he laughed.

Within the hour, we were preparing to clear our new objective, a mosque suspected of being used as an insurgent stronghold. Second Platoon was tasked with actually seizing the building. They initially met light resistance, but it faded into the city once the tanks arrived on scene. We used an Abrams main gun round to breach the outer wall of the compound. The company was able to secure the building without injury quickly.

Shortly after our reconsolidation within the

building, the tanks had to pull back to refuel, leaving the company alone. We didn't have to wait long for the insurgent response. They quickly began to swarm the buildings surrounding the compound, placing heavy, accurate fire on our new position.

We had two sniper teams working targets on the upper floor of the mosque. Cpl. Ziolkowski and Cpl. Esquibel, along with their respective teams, were desperately trying to keep the enemy off us. There were few places within the compound from which we could fire, so most of the company just sat inside the main building and listened to the gunfight above us.

The mosque's main building was an open floor plan with a raised pulpit in the center. The floors had green carpets, and dark-green trim adorned the walls. A large dome on the roof covered the main floor. A balcony served as the second floor. This balcony was where the sniper battle was taking place.

Laforce placed me in a position on a first-floor window that overlooked an entrance on the courtyard's west side. I sat my assault pack down and rested the muzzle of my M16 on the window. I sat on watch from this window for two hours without seeing a single thing. The high walls of the courtyard shielded me from the gunfire from the adjacent buildings.

After two hours, my back teeth were swimming because I had to pee so bad. I asked one of the nearby marines from the scout sniper security section to take my place to relieve myself into an empty water bottle. He sat down, and I began to walk away. I took about three steps before I heard him fire a three-round burst. I spun around and saw him staring down his gunsights. A man lay dead in the courtyard entrance. I had just spent two hours staring at an insurgent wearing black.

After I relieved myself, I went back to the window. Someone had removed the body and closed the door again. I didn't see anything else for the next hour that I sat there. The sun soon began to set, but the gunfire from the rooftop didn't let up. The sniper teams were still engaging targets.

One of the company's interpreters had found a small radio somewhere in the building. He had been listening to news reports on the Baghdad channels. The news soon ended, and music began to play. Celine Dion's "My Heart Will Go On" began to fill the air. One of the marines turned the volume on full blast so everyone could hear the music.

The sun had almost entirely set. The dark room was filled with dirty, exhausted marines. Nobody spoke; we all sat and listened. One man began to sing along, then another. Soon a whole chorus of marines was sitting in the dark in downtown Fallujah singing "Near, far, wherever you are . . ."

"Shut that gay shit off," a voice bellowed above the chorus. It was GySgt. Brown, from the weapons platoon. His voice brought everyone back to reality. The music was quickly turned off.

The firing died down once it got too dark to see. The enemy didn't have enough night-vision capabilities to outfit everyone. It was also too dangerous for them to move around at night because we could easily spot them from the air. AC-130 "Spooky" gunships came on station once the sun had set. These airplane fortresses could see everything moving in the streets below and target it with their 25 mm cannons.

Shortly after nightfall, the company prepared to move out. Each platoon was to continue its movement south. Third Platoon's objective was a large house several hundred meters from the mosque. We moved out first. First Platoon and Second Platoon moved to their objectives several minutes later. We reached our building without incident. The company headquarters section traveled with us, as well as a section each of AAVs and tanks.

The tanks used their main gun rounds to shoot a hole in the courtyard so we could enter. A bomb had partially destroyed the house, but it was a large building even with the damage. We could access only half the house due to the damages and couldn't get on the roof. I sat in a dining room chair and began to pull security out a window. I listened to Capt. Omohundro, the first sergeant, and Lt. Wilkens discuss alternate locations.

"There's somebody in the house—quiet," someone hissed. I listened but couldn't hear anything.

Capt. Omohundro turned to Lt. Wilkens and told him to get moving. It seemed we weren't waiting around to see if we indeed did have houseguests. We quickly exited the house. The damage to the structure and our inability to access the roof made the position untenable. We moved down the street to another, more secure building.

The platoon was lined up in the street; the tank had fired its main gun round into the new building to clear it out and give us a new entry hole. It was taking several minutes for the marines to crawl through the hole and clear the house. Those of us not involved in the clearance waited outside.

Third Squad was last in the order of movement. I was the point man for the squad. Immediately in front of me was the headquarters section and the FiST. I was half-asleep and droning as I stood there. Due to my fatigue, I was standing too close to the marine in front of me. It was dark, so I couldn't tell who it was, but I thought he was a lieutenant from the FiST.

A machine gun opened up off to my right, from my two o'clock position. I watched in horror as a tracer flew from the gun. It traveled between myself and the man in front of me before striking the wall and ricocheting. The glowing round seemed to splinter after hitting the wall. A piece flew straight toward the man in front of me. I heard the round thump as it penetrated his leg. He dropped with a groan.

I was too stunned to move. The communications NCO was standing in front of the stricken man. He turned, scooped the wounded man into his arms, and ran toward the breach site. A burst of machine-gun fire from a nearby AAV silenced the enemy gun as I quickly followed the rest of the platoon into the building.

We established security in the building and passed the rest of the night without incident. First Platoon was not so lucky. They had received contact as they'd moved through the quiet streets. By dawn, one marine was dead, two more were injured, and one had earned himself the Navy Cross.

Sgt. Aubrey McDade was a machine gun squad leader in First Platoon. Insurgents had ambushed his platoon while they had been making their way down Fallujah's dark streets. Cpl. Nathan Anderson and two other marines had been shot. McDade had risked his own life by braving the hail of enemy gunfire to drag those two men out of the kill zone. Anderson had not survived his injuries. The Marine Corps decorated Sgt. McDade with the country's second-highest award for valor: the Navy Cross.

CHAPTER 12

The morning of November 12 was like every other morning during the battle. We woke up just before sunrise and went on 100 percent security. We called this the *morning stand-to*. Lt. Wilkens would receive the day's objective from the company commander. We had changed up our movement technique due to enemy contact. We began to use a bounding overwatch technique to move. One platoon would cover the movement of the others. The moving platoons would then establish an overwatch position for the first platoon.

We soon received our orders to continue selectively clearing south. Our platoon had moved only a block when we began to receive AK-47 fire from a nearby rooftop. I crouched inside a building while Second Squad tried to determine where the fire was coming from.

Between the First Battle of Fallujah in April 2004 and the second battle in November, the insurgents had fortified many buildings. The insurgent holding up our platoon movement was using one of those fortified positions to fire on us. The fighter had knocked a hole in the wall on one of the flat rooftops. He was approximately 250 feet away from our position. His fields of fire controlled all the alleyways around the nearby buildings. We had to take him out.

"Get me two AT4s!" I heard Lt. Wilkens shout. I had been lugging around a heavy AT4 anti-tank rocket since the start of the battle. I jumped at the chance to lighten my load. I shouted to Laforce that I was going upstairs to help as I ran past him. Cpl. Straub, a team leader from Second Squad, also ran upstairs with a rocket.

I quickly found myself crouching next to Straub and Lt. Wilkens behind a rooftop wall. Lt. Wilkens directed us onto our target as we snuck glances over the wall. He wanted us to both fire at the same time. The technique, called a volley fire, was intended to ensure the destruction of the target. The man we were targeting fired occasionally, letting us know he was still there.

We both prepped our rockets. To put effective rounds on the target, we had to expose ourselves to his fire. I fully expected to eat a face full of lead when we stood up. My fists clenched around the sling supporting the rocket tube as I readied myself to fire.

"On three," Straub whispered. His clenched fists and the tone of his voice indicated that he had the same reservations as I did. "One, two, three," he counted.

On his count of three, I quickly rose to my feet. I lined the front sight onto my target and depressed the red trigger. I felt the firing mechanism engage and almost simultaneously felt the weapon fire. The noise was tremendous.

I felt as if a giant hand slapped my back and legs. The pressure from the backblast kicked up dust and debris, which hammered against me. I watched as the small hole in the rooftop I was aiming toward exploded in fire, smoke, and dust.

Straub stood beside me, attempting remedial action on his launcher. It had failed to fire. This was a common problem with the AT4s the marines issued us. The fire from the opposing rooftop had stopped. The wall had completely collapsed, and dust hung thick in the air.

"Good job, guys!" Lt. Wilkens shouted to us. "I think you got him. Go throw those tubes in the streets for the tanks to run over. I'll have Llerena shoot a S.M.A.W. into it for good measure, just in case."

Before walking downstairs, I glanced back at the smoldering wreckage. I saw no sign of movement from its previous occupant. My movements were robotic as I carried my spent launcher down to the street for the tanks to crush. We had to destroy them since we couldn't reuse them and because the insurgents could use the spent launchers to shoot mortars or pack improvised explosive devices into.

After I returned home, a friend once asked me what it was like to shoot at someone. I felt nothing when I stepped off that rooftop. My feelings about this incident have never changed. I will atone for my sins one day, but I feel no remorse or regret. It was just a thing that happened.

We continued with our journey south. After advancing a couple of blocks, we prepared to enter another courtyard. The courtyards all had metal gates blocking their driveways. We would have to breach those gates, then clear the courtyard. Only once we had a foothold in the courtyard could we make entry into the houses. Every house we cleared was a mini fortress with multiple levels of defense.

First Squad made entry into this particular courtyard and began to sweep for the enemy. Inside the courtyard, we found the 82 mm mortar that had been fired on us two days before. There was also a ZPU-1 antiaircraft gun. After clearing the rest of the building, we took turns playing with the antiaircraft gun while Lt. Wilkens figured out our next move. We gave the grid coordinates to the battalion headquarters so they could target the weapons systems. Then we made our way to another two-story house, where we made our patrol base for the night.

We received word that an army unit, 1-5 Cavalry, First Cavalry Division, would be clearing through our position that night. Their task was to use their M2 Bradley infantry fighting vehicles to draw enemy fire as they drove down the street. They could then use their 30 mm guns to target these enemy positions and eliminate them. We marked our positions with VS-17 panels and IR strobes. They passed through our lines without incident. We could hear Bradley's engaging targets for several hours through the night.

The battle reached a turning point after the twelfth of November. US forces had seized the center of the city, and the enemy tactics had begun to change. They no longer attacked us whenever we moved, but they instead began sniping us from afar and ambushing us when we were inside their buildings. Our artillery and tanks had decimated their numbers. Instead of resisting us openly, they began to ambush us in the streets or the houses. They waited until we were too close to call in our overwhelming firepower. We had no choice but to slug it out from ranges of less than twenty feet.

The morning of November 13 was clear and crisp. We began to make our way south, encountering only sporadic gunfire. We cleared several blocks without incident when we found a cache of land mines in one of the houses. Around one hundred mines were lying in boxes around the residence—everything from anti-tank mines to anti-personnel mines.

We set up a security perimeter and called the company commander to report our find. He radioed back to tell us an Explosive Ordinance Disposal (EOD) team was heading our way to dispose of the land mines. It would take several hours for them to arrive, though.

Second Squad was told to secure the kitchen and backside of the complex. Sgt. Hayden put Neely and his M249 SAW in an overwatch position at the back door. Neely pulled a chair from the kitchen table and sat in it, his SAW barrel propped up in the windowsill. The rest of us found places to sit down wherever we could. The weight of my plates and assault pack was killing my shoulders. I found a seat on a nearby milk crate and waited for the inevitable order to move again.

The entire platoon began to get some much-needed rest. All of us were exhausted from the past five days of fighting. I sat in the kitchen and watched the faces of those around me. Houck was leaning back against a bag of rice. His blue eyes appeared to focus on something far away, yet he was staring at the wall across the room. Nobody spoke; every man was lost in his thoughts. Bowman lit a cigarette and slowly puffed on it. The attached photographer snapped pictures of us sitting there. I would later learn that one of the images he took of me ended up in my hometown newspaper back in Canandaigua.

We took turns rotating through the security position at the back door. Eventually, a convoy containing the EOD team pulled up to the front of the home. The engineer in charge examined our find for several minutes. I overheard him telling Lt. Wilkens the mines were Italian made. He directed us to move the land mines to the back of an empty five-ton truck.

We began to stack the mines into the truck. They were VS-2.2 land mines, sold to the Iraqis during the Iran-Iraq War. They were tan-colored circular mines that weighed about seven pounds. The mines were designed to disable armored vehicles. It took us the better part of thirty minutes to load all the land mines into the truck.

"I wouldn't want to be driving this thing," Holmes joked as we closed the tailgate on a truck bed full of land mines. I laughed, thinking that the driver must be crazy to drive that many explosives through the city streets.

Once we loaded the truck, the EOD team began the long drive back to Camp Fallujah to dispose of the ordnance. After they left, we prepared to move out. GySgt. Parry told Sgt. Hayden that Third Squad was taking point. It was early afternoon; we had wasted most of the day waiting on EOD to remove the land mines.

We moved two blocks south before we encountered a house adjacent to a vacant field. We established an overwatch position while First Squad moved in to clear it. Inside the courtyard, we found a tunnel dug into the dirt. It led underneath the street. Our intelligence section had warned us that the insurgents had constructed these tunnel networks to move between buildings. The tunnels allowed them to avoid being sighted by our aircraft. We cleared the tunnel but found nothing.

We found evidence that people had been inside the house recently. We could always tell when an insurgent group had stayed in a home because they left their sleeping mats underneath the windows and doors. We assumed they did this as an early warning as someone jumping through the window would land on the sleeping person.

It was getting dark, and the order came down to establish our patrol base for the night. We set up in a two-story building, and each squad was assigned a sector to cover. Sgt. Hayden established a watch rotation while we all tried to find a good place to sleep. Houck, Laforce, and Neely ended up sharing a bed in the master bedroom while I took a sleeping mat out of the closet to use. I glanced at my watch; it was 2230. My shift wasn't until 0100. I looked forward to nearly two hours of uninterrupted sleep. I hadn't been out of my uniform since the start of the battle, and my pants were so stiff from all the sweat that it was uncomfortable. I pulled them off and slid under my poncho liner. In a matter of minutes I was soundly sleeping.

Houck woke me up five minutes before the start of my watch shift, and it took me a second to realize what was happening. He motioned towards a window where he had been standing guard. He told me it had been a quiet night. There had been gunfire several blocks away, but nothing directed at us, and he hadn't seen any movement in the streets below. After he was satisfied that I wouldn't fall back asleep, he moved back to his window position.

I didn't even bother putting my pants back on. I wiped the sleep from my eyes and threw my IBA on over my T-shirt. I quickly grabbed my poncho liner and rifle before shuffling over to Houck's position. He was sitting on an MRE box at a windowsill on the second floor. The window overlooked the courtyard and the street below. He stood up when I got there and grinned when he saw my bare legs in the moonlight.

"Don't ask, man," I mumbled.

"Wasn't going to," he replied before walking to bed.

I plopped down on the box. I rested my rifle barrel on the windowsill and took stock of the position. The moonlight illuminated the ground outside. I could see the top of the brick wall surrounding the courtyard. There was broken glass laid into the mortar on top of the wall—I could see it glistening in the moonlight. I surmised it served the purpose of barbed wire, prohibiting intruders from jumping the fence without cutting themselves.

I looked around me. I was alone in the room. I could hear my squadmates snoring in the bedroom next door and the shuffling and murmured voices of other marines on watch on the floors below me.

Thoughts of home began to flood my mind. I thought of everything I would miss out on if I got killed. Every hope, every dream, every aspiration I ever had would die with me. I would never get to be a father, never hold another woman, and never have sex again. Sitting there alone with no distraction allowed my mind to run wild. I was exhausted and was fighting back the sleep that my body so desperately needed.

I had just gotten comfortable when all hell broke loose. Gunfire erupted from a building a block north of us. The fire peppered the walls surrounding my perch with bullets. I quickly forgot about my activities and grabbed my rifle. My eyes searched for a target. I could hear GySgt. Parry screaming for everyone to stand-to. Marines were scrambling to man every window.

"Hold your fire!" Lt. Wilkens screamed out. "There's an Iraqi Army unit near there, and I think it may be friendly fire." The shooting died down as quickly as it had begun. I assumed that the company headquarters had reached out to the marine advisors attached to the Iraqi units to stop the shooting.

Another ten minutes passed before GySgt. Parry would let everyone go back to sleep. He glanced at me as he walked by. I was sitting on an MRE box in boxers, a T-shirt, my IBA, and Kevlar. "What the fuck?" was all he muttered in response to my state of dress.

I soon found myself alone again at my windowsill perch. I glanced at my watch; I had twenty more minutes. I spent the rest of my shift in silence before waking Neely up for his turn. Once I was relieved, I crawled back onto my commandeered mat and fell asleep. The rest of the night passed without incident.

I watched the sunrise on November 14 while

perched in a different windowsill in the house. The entire platoon had been awake before the sun rose so we could conduct stand-to. We conducted stand-to every morning while out on patrol. It involved everyone waking up before the sunrise and preparing to repel a dawn attack. The purpose of stand-to was to prevent surprise attacks on a sleeping force. Our morning stand-to passed without incident.

We prepared to continue our movement south. We had reached the edge of the city's residential district and were beginning to enter the Jubail District. The buildings were spaced out more, which allowed for enemy forces to engage us at longer distances. It also meant our tank support had more room to maneuver.

We left our patrol base in a column formation. Second Squad took point, followed by Third, then First. First Platoon reported heavy contact, and we moved to support them. First's position was less than a block from ours, and we made it there within minutes. We encountered no resistance on our route. By the time we got there, the contact had died down.

They had occupied a building at the southern edge of the residential district. It was a typical building surrounded by a brick-walled courtyard. First already had security, so our platoon filed into the lower floor of the house. Lt. Wilkens linked up with Capt. Omohundro and Lt. Berch to discuss the company's movement into the less densely packed southern districts.

I sat against a wall next to Laforce; it felt good to get the weight of my assault pack off my shoulders. I placed my Kevlar helmet underneath my pack to hold the weight up, then looked around the room at the marines seated alongside me. Some were talking among themselves; most were smoking cigarettes. I was beginning to feel that I may make it out of Fallujah unharmed. It had been several days since our last casualty, and it seemed that we had broken the back of most enemy resistance.

I closed my eyes and tried to imagine what was happening back home. Deer season would be in full swing. Dad's collision shop would probably be packed with crashed cars from all the deer moving. They'd probably already had their first frost of the year. I wished I were back home—anywhere but here.

My daydream was cut short by the crack of a single rifle shot. We all snapped awake; the talking stopped. The marines on the roof answered with shouts and a burst of automatic weapons fire.

"Corpsman!" The shout resonated from the rooftop. I knew it could mean only one thing; this fight was far from decided. There was a burst of movement as several marines rushed upstairs to help. The shooting quickly died down.

Several marines began to bring the casualty downstairs. The rest of us sat silently, watching the macabre procession. They were using a poncho as a litter. The man had been shot in the head; I couldn't discern who it was from his disfigured face. It was immediately apparent that the corpsman could do nothing to help him.

"They fucking shot Ski," Landers mumbled. I looked at the limp form. He was one of our scout snipers, Cpl. Nicholas Ziolkowski. He was one of the best snipers in the battalion. They laid his body on the floor while we waited for the medevac track to arrive. Nobody spoke; the silence was deafening.

The sounds of the approaching vehicles broke the silence. Several men stood and loaded Ski's body into the waiting vehicles. I could tell by the slowly fading sounds of their engines they were heading back toward Camp Fallujah. Soon the room was plunged back into silence.

I looked around the room again. Every single man in that room was staring into nothing. Everyone's eyes seemed to be focused on some distant object, and their faces were expressionless. The exhaustion was clear in the features of everyone. Some smoked cigarettes; others just stared. We were all contemplating our fates.

I began to think that perhaps it would be better if I could just get shot. I silently prayed to God, asking if he would allow me to get wounded. I figured getting myself a slight wound would be better than facing death. I contemplated the benefits of getting maimed for several minutes before deciding that I couldn't control whether I got hit.

Nobody had that much control over their lives. It all came down to luck.

My thoughts were soon interrupted by GySgt. Parry telling us to get ready. We were going to continue our movement south. First Platoon would provide overwatch to cover our movement. Our objective was another residence three blocks south in the area of First Platoon's morning firefight.

We came into contact as soon as we got close to our objective. Lt. Wilkens ordered us to clear a home while we waited for tank support. This building was a little different than the others in that it didn't have a courtyard surrounding it. The entrance opened onto the street. We quickly established a base of fire for the other platoons in the company to maneuver against the enemy positions.

Most of my platoon made their way upstairs to get a better vantage point to fire on the enemy positions. Laforce ordered me to stay in the front room to guard the entrance onto the street. I stood in the front sitting room, guarding the door, when I heard the unmistakable whirring sound of tank engines outside. The Abrams stopped directly in front of our building. I could see it through the window; its gun barrel was scanning for targets. The crescendo of gunfire from upstairs increased.

I was surprised when the tank fired its main gun round. The enormous back pressure created by the round blew the windows out. The curtains were sucked out with the glass. I felt the pressure course through my body. My ears began to ring as all other sounds were drowned out. I staggered over to a couch and sat down. It took several minutes for the ringing in my ears to die down. The tank moved on several minutes after firing.

Within an hour, the shooting died down. The tank support had driven the enemy back into their remaining strongholds in the city's southern edge. The coalition had secured most of the city, and the remaining enemy fighters were mainly trying to flee the fighting by crossing the Euphrates. Those who remained were there to fight to the death. We began to move south again, into the less densely packed southern edge of the city.

Lt. Wilkens selected a sizeable two-story house as our base of operations for the night. Battalion assigned a section of tanks to the platoon for the evening. They established themselves in the streets outside of our location. Tanks had a weakness in an urban environment—they had blind spots where their optics could not see, especially in the complex terrain associated with multi-floor buildings. GySgt. Parry established a watch rotation between the different fire teams, and we took turns providing overwatch on the tanks throughout the night.

CHAPTER 13

Just before dawn on November 15, GySgt. Parry woke the entire platoon for stand-to. Cpl. Straub noticed four men low crawling near our position. He fired on the men, wounding one and causing the others to surrender.

The men looked to be in their mid-twenties. They were wearing running shoes, a sign that they were fighters. Most of the civilians we encountered wore sandals. Sandals seemed to be the universal footwear of choice in Al Anbar. Only those involved in the fighting wore sneakers, which allowed them to move around better than they could in traditional sandals. Unfortunately for them, it also made them stand out in a crowd. Another dead giveaway was the AK-47s we found discarded near their positions.

When questioned, they said they were going to school. No schools were operating due to the heavy fighting, and they couldn't even tell us where their school was. Straub was talking to them through Ajax, our interpreter. He relayed their message of traveling to school to Lt. Wilkens.

"Yeah, Jihad University," someone quipped.

We treated the wounded fighter before sending him back to the battalion aid station for medical treatment. We had no facilities to hold any detainees, nor did we have the training necessary to question them. All we could do was search them, safeguard them, then speed them to the rear for intelligence processing.

We soon received orders to continue into the Shuhada District, the southernmost district in the city. We were several blocks from the edge of the city and presumably near the end of the fighting. The enemy had begun to hide inside buildings at this point, fighting us only when we entered the houses they were sheltering inside.

Each squad would clear a building independently of the others. First Squad would clear the first building; Second would take the next, followed by Third. Spreading out would allow us to cover more ground. If a squad got into contact, we would all converge on the sounds of their guns. We were never out of hearing range of the other squads. This minimized the risks that the enemy could cut a squad off from the platoon.

Second Squad had just finished clearing our assigned house. We had ended before the other two squads, so we had time to kill. I was sitting down on a couch when I heard an explosion from the house next door. The explosion was quickly followed up with the cry of "Corpsman!"

We rushed outside to see what was going on. I ran into the courtyard and saw blood everywhere. Parker was lying on the ground; his chest was ripped open. Doc Masino knelt over him, but it was clearly too late. The explosion had torn his body open, killing him instantly. He was eighteen years old.

We never discerned what exactly caused the explosion that killed him. The best we could determine was that he had triggered a grenade, either through a tripwire or command detonation. We had to keep moving, so we didn't have much time to investigate. We loaded him into an AAV, and we moved on.

We continued to clear south. Within an hour, we found ourselves clearing a mosque at the southern edge of the Shuhada District. We were four blocks from the edge of the city. The mosque was a simple compound, with an outer wall surrounding a courtyard and a garden. The main building was built of white marble. A minaret stood off from the main building, towering about thirty feet in the air. The minaret had a spiraling staircase inside, which led to a window near the top. It overlooked a broad field that separated the Shuhada and Jubail Districts of the city.

We quickly cleared the courtyard and mosque. The final area that we needed to clear was the minaret, which was cleared by Houck and Bowman. At the top, they found the corpse of an enemy fighter buried in the rubble. The minaret had been hit by a tank main gun round, which had killed him. The fact that there was a dead man at the top wasn't unique; what was notable was his skin color. He was a black man of African descent. The intelligence section had warned us of foreign fighters operating in the city, but this was the first time we could conclusively prove it. Bowman snapped a picture with his digital camera.

Shortly after we cleared the compound, we got the order to move out. We began to take enemy small arms fire as soon as we left the safety of the walls. The platoon was able to make the last four blocks without taking casualties. We linked up with the company headquarters section and the FiST in a home at the city's edge. Second Squad was put on rest for a few hours, so we made ourselves at home in one of the upstairs bedrooms. We were excited about making it to the edge of the city, and we all hoped we would be relieved soon.

Our rest was short-lived. Lt. Wilkens came into the room to tell us that Alpha Company had taken a casualty, and they needed us to escort the battalion chaplain to their position. They were located a block to our west. Lt. Wilkens tasked our fire team with providing the escort. We quickly checked our ammunition and prepared to head out. Lt. Wilkens and his RTO, LCpl. Cullen Fitchett, came along with us to ensure we got there in one piece.

Alpha Company's position wasn't too far from our location, but we didn't know exactly where they were. We crept out and made our way down the street. The sound of gunfire reverberated from the houses up ahead. We knew that enemy fighters were in the buildings adjacent to us, so we couldn't just walk up and see if Alpha was there. We made our way to a fighting position that someone had dug near a wall. It was only big enough for four of us. Chaplain Cox and Lt. Wilkens stayed outside while Fitchett made radio contact with Alpha's headquarters.

As we tried to gain radio contact, a MARPAT-covered helmet popped up over the roof of the building adjacent to us. It was a marine from Alpha Company. He stared at us for a second before yelling, "What the fuck are you guys doing down there?"

We yelled back about delivering Chaplain Cox. The marine told us to take cover; the building directly across the street was filled with insurgents who had just killed a marine. Alpha Company was about to launch a SMAW rocket into the building, and we were directly underneath the SMAW gunner. We made ourselves as small as we could in the hole as we waited for the explosion. I was pressed tightly between Neely and Houck. Lt. Wilkens and the chaplain squeezed into the hole as best they could.

I heard the rocket launch, followed by a massive explosion as the thermobaric round detonated inside the building. We were all shaken up but otherwise unscathed. Lt. Wilkens, Fitchett, and Chaplain Cox ran into the building to link up with Alpha Company while the rest of us stayed in the fighting position. We warily eyed the smoking ruins of the house across the street while we waited for Lt. Wilkens and Fitchett to return. Within a few minutes, they returned, and we quickly made our way back to the rest of the platoon.

When we got back, the rest of my squad was still resting where we had left them. About an hour after we got back, a colonel and his entourage stopped by the position. He began to talk with us, asking about the fighting. Laforce told him it was my twentieth birthday.

He looked at me, smiled, and said, "Just think—next year, you'll be able to buy a beer."

I smiled politely as he moved on. I was indifferent about my birthday or his presence among us, for that matter. He didn't stay with us long. Once he left, we went back to sitting on our packs.

Bowman and Houck began telling everyone about their find in the minaret earlier in the morning. Bowman handed around his digital camera to show us the evidence. I stared at the grainy image of the dead man. He had a close-cropped beard and curly black hair. The dust from the debris had powdered his dark face. His eyes were opened but not focused on anything. I wondered what had caused him to come all this way to die.

The *New York Times* reporter and photographer joined us in the room as I looked at the camera. I remembered them telling us several days before that they had been looking for evidence of foreign involvement in the fighting. I figured that this picture would interest them.

"Check this out," I said as I handed the camera over. "You wanted to see a dead foreigner; well, at least I don't think he looks like a local. Do you?"

"Where'd you find him?" Gilbertson asked as he looked over the photo.

"He's in that minaret up the road," I told him, pointing to the tower visible out the window.

The two men quickly left the room. They wanted to see the man for themselves so that they could get pictures for their paper, so they asked Capt. Omohundro if they could see for themselves. He detailed a squad from First Platoon to go with them.

I was simply happy Second Squad didn't have to go. I would get to catch up on some much-needed sleep. I lay back and closed my eyes as I heard First Platoon beginning to move out. I quickly drifted off.

I wasn't asleep long before the sound of gunfire awoke me. It was coming from the mosque. Voices on the radio exploded in activity. I knew instantly that First Platoon had made contact, and it didn't sound good.

The platoon commander tasked a fire team to reclear the minaret. LCpl. Billy Miller took point. He was a twenty-two-year-old marine from Pearland, Texas. Following him was LCpl. Christian Dominguez, then the photographer Ashley Gilbertson. Unbeknown to them, an enemy sniper had reoccupied the minaret. As Miller and Dominguez had neared the top of the steps, they had come face to face with this enemy fighter.

The insurgent had gotten the drop on them. Miller had been shot and had fallen back down the stairs. The men had beat a hasty retreat, bringing Miller out with them. They pulled out of the compound while the FiST called in an airstrike on the position. We all watched as the plane came in and dropped its payload. The minaret crumbled under the explosions. Nobody else would be occupying that tower to shoot at marines.

Later that evening, I was posted on guard duty on the rooftop. Landers and I sat and watched the sunset over the Iraq desert. To our north, smoke rose from various parts of the city. The streets were no longer navigable to wheeled traffic; the debris and destruction of war had blocked them. The power lines were hanging in the streets, and you would have to search for several hours to find a building that wasn't damaged.

The *New York Times* reporter was sitting near us, trying to get a signal to send out his stories. He looked at me and asked what I had gotten for my birthday. I didn't even look at him when I said, "Two dead friends." I knew it would be many years before I celebrated my birthday again, assuming I made it past the next few weeks.

We spent that night in the house on the southern edge of the city. The fighting would continue for several more weeks, but there was little doubt that we had secured Fallujah. There would be no political interference that the insurgents could use to claim victory.

CHAPTER 14

We left our position early in the morning on November 16. We had slogged our way from north to south and had run out of city to seize. Our new task was to mop up the remaining fighters. Instead of selectively clearing critical points in the city, we now systematically cleared every house. We moved to a school in the southern part of the city to establish our company base. We would spend the next several days rotating through pulling security on the school while the other two platoons cleared every home in the city's southern area. The *New York Times* reporters left shortly after Miller got killed.

Third Platoon spent most of November 16 digging positions and filling sandbags at the school. The school wasn't that big. It was a two-story circular building with a courtyard in the center. The classrooms opened into an open-air hallway that overlooked the courtyard. We placed a machine-gun position on the roof, protected with sandbags filled with earth from the yard. Originally, this position was occupied by an M240. We later supplemented it with an M2 .50 cal. we found hidden under a bag of dates in a storage shed.

We placed guards along each wall. The scout snipers established various positions throughout the building, which gave them fields of fire down all avenues of approach. Our mortar section set a 60 mm mortar in the front of the building. We used the dirt from the mortar pit to help fill the sandbags. Digging in the rocky sand was grueling labor, but at least we were in the relative safety of the school's walls.

The company spent most of the day digging in, with no enemy contact. By the early evening, we were safely ensconced behind our defenses. The forward support company was able to bring us hot chow for the first time since the battle began. The hot food was a great morale booster after the stressful fight. Houck raised a wooden flagpole in the center of the courtyard with a green sandbag attached to it. Inscribed on the sandbag were the names of our dead.

I was placed on guard duty on the western wall. I sat in a white plastic lawn chair and watched the sunset over the top of the city. Across the street from the school were the remains of two enemy fighters. I studied them in the dwindling daylight. Their blackened and bloated corpses contrasted with the white robes they wore. I could see the flies buzzing around their remains. I felt nothing toward them; they were just another casualty in this grizzly city.

Third Platoon wasn't assigned to patrol on the seventeenth either. First and Second set off early in the morning to clear their assigned sectors. Third Platoon had to unload C-wire from the back of an LMTV. More engineers had augmented our company. We were using the C-wire to create an impenetrable barrier around the walls of the school. It would prevent enemy fighters from infiltrating our positions.

While we unloaded the wire, Hayden told Laforce to have the team clear the area immediately around the school compound. We would be exposed as we moved and emplaced the wire, and we needed to be sure that nobody was in the adjacent buildings. We moved out and began to clear the surrounding area hastily. As we walked, I noticed an enemy fighting position overlooking the school's southern side. If an enemy got into the position, they would fire on our entrance control point. We quickly radioed the location to Lt. Wilkens; he had the engineers bulldoze the fighting position. We cleared the rest of the perimeter without incident.

Later that afternoon, we each got to make a phone call using the company's satellite phone. Each marine in the company took turns using it for a five-minute phone call. I tried calling my dad, but he didn't answer. I finally got ahold of my mom. I tried to deflect her questions; I didn't want her to worry. She began to tell me how my picture had been in the local newspaper. Ashley Gilbertson had photographed me, and his photo had gotten picked up by the Rochester, New York, newspaper the *Democrat and Chronicle*. Mom tried to explain this to me when the snipers began to engage a target from the rooftop above me. Mom asked what the noise was. I lied and said they were just sighting in their guns. The connection went dead several seconds later. I didn't bother calling back. I had nothing to talk about.

I went back to the perimeter to help lay wire. Holmes struggled with opening up a coil of C-wire, so I walked over to lend a hand. I told him how my picture had made the newspaper in my hometown. I asked if he had gotten to make a phone call. He told me how he had called his brother earlier in the morning. I could tell from the tone of his voice that he was homesick; he seemed to be talking more for his benefit than mine.

We talked about home and how we couldn't wait to get back to it as we continued laying the wire around the school's perimeter. The days were beginning to cool off, so the oppressive heat we had experienced during the summer wasn't much of a factor. We worked throughout the rest of the afternoon. The patrols from the other platoons came in as the sun began to set. They brought with them the various weapons they had found hidden among the houses in the area. The commander had them laid out in the quad of the school. We spent the evening walking through the growing piles of automatic rifles like kids in a candy store. The discarded weapons were the closest many of us had ever been to PKMs, RPKs, Dragunovs, and RPG launchers.

Third Platoon wasn't sent out on the eighteenth either. We spent the day laying more wire and continuing to fortify the company's position. The only incident of note was that a news crew from Al Jazeera came into the school. They spent the day filming us as we went about fortifying our positions. They didn't talk to us much; they only took photos and filmed.

In the early afternoon, I was helping the mortar section dig in their firing pit. We were discussing the battle and how crazy things had gotten when I heard a shuffling sound from the rooftop above us. I looked up and found that the Al Jazeera crew had their cameras trained on us. They had been secretly filming us from the second-floor balcony of the school. Their presence put a damper on the conversation. We continued to dig in silence. The film crew left the company's position later that evening.

Sgt. Hayden brought the whole squad together after dinner to brief us on our patrol route for the nineteenth. The commander assigned my platoon to clear a sector of houses several blocks away. We had one day to clear around seventy-five homes. Lt. Wilkens planned on the squads leapfrogging each other as we cleared houses. Spreading out would allow us to clear three places simultaneously while still maintaining contact with each other if needed. The risks of enemy contact were high; the reports we were getting in from battalion were that enemy fighters had gone to ground in the homes and were ambushing marine units as they cleared through.

We started our movement before the sun came up. The streets had been destroyed. Large craters left pockmarks in the roadway. Telephone and electric wires hung low across the road since the explosions had snapped the telephone poles. The streets were hardly navigable to wheeled traffic due to all the rubble—not that there was any traffic except the occasional US tank or AAV. Almost every building had structural damage from the heavy fighting.

We were in our search area a little after dawn. The first few houses we entered were dry holes for anything of military value. The homes were filled with the usual knickknacks you would find in any home; family pictures, kids' toys, and furniture. The owners had taken everything of real value—not that we were looking to take things. Our primary concern was finding weapons caches to inhibit the Mujahedin's ability to continue fighting.

After searching through several homes, we finally found what we were looking for. Cpl. Laforce and Cpl. Landers looked underneath a mattress and saw what looked like several rifles. Landers flipped the bed and found four AK-47 rifles and several loaded magazines. It was a small cache but was more than we had expected to find in one house. First and Second Squads also found weapons in the adjacent houses, confirming our suspicions that enemy fighters were operating in the immediate area.

The walled courtyards created miniature fortresses around the homes. A city block may have had ten buildings connected through their walled courtyards. The Mujahedin would create holes from courtyard to courtyard, then hide weapons throughout the block. These caches allowed them to fire on US forces before dropping their weapons and falling back on another supply. They knew that we couldn't fire if we didn't see a gun and didn't have hostile intent.

We continued searching for weapons as we cleared our sector. We heard radio traffic that First Platoon was in contact. There was an ever-present sound of gunfire throughout the city; it never seemed to die down or go away. We could do little for the marines in First Platoon, so we continued clearing our assigned sector.

It took us most of the day to clear our sector. We made our way back to the company combat outpost as the sun was beginning to set. Almost every marine carried an extra weapon liberated from the Mujahedin caches. These weapons would be added to the growing pile in the courtyard of the school. We appeared to be measuring success by the size of the weapons pile in front of the company headquarters.

After we got back, we linked up with the marines in First Platoon. We learned that LCpl. Demarcus Brown and LCpl. Demetri Gavriel had been killed in an ambush. They had entered a house to clear it when the Mujahedin opened fire on them. Brown had made it out of the building only to succumb to his wounds in the aid station. Gavriel had never made it out. Their deaths stunned us; both had been well-liked men in the company. The atmosphere in the company that night was depressed and melancholy. We knew that there would be more casualties as we continued our clearing operations. Houck added their names to the growing list on his sandbag flag in the courtyard.

CHAPTER 15

The morning of November 20 found us again on patrol. We snaked our way through the devastated city shortly after dawn, quietly moving to our assigned search area. The squads split up and began systematically clearing each house in our sector. We quickly started finding weapons hidden in the homes. I could tell that people had been in the homes recently because they had left their sleeping mats underneath the windows. Sleeping under the window would both allow them an easy escape if needed and would also help them know if someone tried to enter through the window.

We were all on edge after what had happened to First Platoon the day before. We had been clearing for several hours when Neely and I found several rifles and grenades hidden behind a couch in one of the homes. We finished clearing the first floor and made our way to the second. I could hear movement on the roof as we stepped up the stairs. Landers's team cleared the second floor as Laforce, Neely, and I crept toward the rooftop.

Cpl. Laforce yelled out a warning once we got up, yet we got no response. We had heard movement, so we knew someone was up there. I imagined they were going to open fire on us as soon as we cleared the doorway. I prepped a grenade, then quickly tossed it around the corner of the door. Everyone tensed up, waiting for it to explode so we could rush the rooftop.

I felt the explosion through the brick wall we were sheltering behind. We quickly rushed into the smoke and dust. Instead of being met with the expected hail of gunfire, we instead were assaulted by feathers flying through the dust. The noise we had heard was a coop filled with doves, and my grenade had scored a direct hit. The air was filled with the gory aftermath. I felt horrified and relieved at the same time. At least there wasn't an enemy fighter waiting for us, but we were professionals and should have known better.

We picked up the weapons we had found and continued moving. We didn't have time to dwell on dead birds. Several houses later, I found myself in another unique situation. As the squad made entry into another home, Cpl. Roop (an attached S.M.A.W. gunner) and I moved around to clear the building's side and back to make sure nobody was there. We were walking in the grass when I felt something hard under my foot. I looked down and saw I was standing on a land mine. I almost shit my pants before realizing it was an anti-tank mine. I didn't weigh enough to set it off.

I yelled for Roop to freeze, which he did. The enemy had laced the entire yard with mines. A typical American technique was to use the AAVs to breach the courtyards' walls to gain access to the buildings. By placing anti-tank mines in the front yard, the enemy had used our techniques against us. Any armored vehicle that breached the outer wall would have detonated one of these land mines.

Sgt. Hayden radioed the location of the minefield to Lt. Wilkens for later destruction. We didn't have the assets to deal with it ourselves. An EOD team would have to come through and destroy the mines. We continued clearing our sector. Afterward, we returned to the outpost at the school. We were exhausted and sweaty, but we could add to the growing pile of weapons in the courtyard.

That evening I walked through this weapons pile. We had found firearms from across the globe. There were former Soviet AK-47s and AK-74s, Second World War vintage Mausers, Enfields, and even a Gewehr 43 from Nazi Germany. The weapons were in various stages of usefulness. Some were just broken down into parts—either from age or battle damage—while others were in perfectly good working order. Some weapons still carried the blood and tissue of their former owners. Alongside the rifles was a section for hand grenades, an area for RPGs, and another for mortars. After less than a week of searching, we had enough munitions to outfit a rifle battalion with small arms, light to medium machine guns, a sniper section, and a full medium mortar platoon.

Later in the evening, we received the news we had all been waiting for. Third Platoon was going to be rotated back to Camp Fallujah in the morning for a chance to restock at the base PX, take a shower, and refit from the equipment we had left behind in the rear. The forward support company would drive us out early the next morning. It would only be for a day, but it would be a day away from the city. That night I drifted off to sleep thinking about the ice-cold Coke I would buy at the PX.

The next morning, we left when the morning resupply convoy went back to Camp Fallujah. We rode in the back of several open-top five-tons, which were escorted by a section of AAVs. Each truck had a marine from the motor transport section in the back for security. I had little faith in this POG's (a derogatory term for non-infantry) ability to hit anything with his rifle from the end of a moving truck.

The ride through the city was uneventful, but it did provide a unique view of the fighting's utter destruction. The trucks had to snake through the holes and debris in the streets. We passed several landmarks that I had seen on our relentless movement south, such as the government complex and the cultural center. The battalion had turned the government complex into their headquarters. I could see the forest of radio antennas poking up through the rooftop from halfway across the city.

We passed the turquoise-blue-topped domes of one of the local mosques. A bomb had destroyed the back of the building. It looked like it had been one of the most beautiful buildings in the city before the fighting had started. It seemed a shame that such a beautiful structure had been sacrificed.

In the back, the motor-T marine was trying to impress us with his war stories, but none of us cared. When he told us how a mortar round had landed near him, Cpl. Silva looked through him before telling him to "shut the fuck up." We continued the rest of the ride in silence. I watched the young man brood in the back corner of the truck as we left the city behind us.

We pulled back into the bivouac area of Camp Fallujah after only a thirty-minute drive. We unloaded the trucks and crowded around GySgt. Parry for instructions. He gave us five hours to shower, get haircuts, shop at the PX, and "beat our dicks" before linking back up at our current location to head back to the city. Before releasing us, he threatened our lives if we were even one minute late.

Houck and I quickly made our way over to the shower area. We wanted to wash and get clean clothes before getting something to eat at the PX. The shower area was a row of tents with massive water blivets outside of them. One tent was to undress in, while another had hot water piped to it. We were the first ones there, so it wasn't crowded.

I hadn't changed my clothes since the start of the battle. The sweat had left white stains on the back of my blouse, and my pants could probably have stood up on their own they were that stiff with sweat. My back was suffering the effects of prickly heat from all the salt in my pores. The hot water on my skin felt amazing. My skin changed color as I scrubbed the dirt off of it. The water running down my face irritated my eyes from all the dust and sweat in my hair.

The clean cammies I put on afterward felt like pajamas compared to the dirty pair I had just taken off. Having a clean set of clothes on and freshly shampooed hair changed my outlook on life. Houck and I then decided to head over to the PX for a hot meal that hadn't just come out of an MRE bag. We walked the half-mile to the PX and found the rest of the platoon had beaten us there. Grimy, long-haired marines were everywhere in the small PX. A gunnery sergeant from the nearby artillery unit was yelling at everyone, saying we smelled and our hair was out of regulations. We mainly ignored him as we bought up everything in sight.

We both got our hair cut at the barbershop and hit up the internet café before returning to the bivouac area. I had received several emails from friends back home, while Houck had received news on his one-year-old daughter. The information from home fed our conversation as we walked back to the battalion area. Houck talked about how excited he was to see his daughter when he got back.

We rode back out to the company outpost with

the evening resupply. Each of the platoons would rotate back similarly over the next several days. We rode out in silence, and our mood collectively began to darken as we approached the edges of the city. Everyone had their heads on a swivel as we entered the desolated streets. Our brief sojourn back into a somewhat civilized life was over; we were back to the city of mosques.

The next two days saw Third Platoon tasked out to improve the school's fortifications and man the perimeter positions. I spent most of my time sitting behind an M240 mounted to a tripod in a sandbagged position on the school's western wall. The position overlooked a street, with the bodies of two enemy fighters rotting in the sun fifty meters from our wire. The men had been killed in the initial phases of the battle. After a week of lying in the street, they were barely recognizable as humans.

Both men lay on their stomachs. One was clad in a dark-blue thobe, a traditional garment worn throughout the region. His white running shoes stood in stark contrast to his blackened, bloated legs protruding from the bottom of his loose thobe. The other wore a black tracksuit. Both men were in the latter stages of decomposition; thick dark liquid ran out of their bodies into the gutter. Both men had initially been armed with AK-47 rifles, which we had added to our collection in the courtyard when we'd first occupied the school. I had no idea who killed those fighters.

We were waiting for the security situation to improve so mortuary affairs could come and bury the fighters.

I sat behind the machine gun and watched the sunset behind the outline of the ruined city. I had to be careful about exposing myself; snipers were still an ever-present threat. I thought of sunsets I had watched back home over Canandaigua Lake. I tried to remember the water glistening in the golden rays of a setting sun. All I could see, though, were the last bits of light casting eerie shadows over my departed companions in the street. Once the darkness set in, I peered through the PAS-13 thermal scope on the gun. The scope provided a thermal image, allowing the gunner to distinguish targets in the night easily. The only thing I could see through the scope was the red heat signature of stray cats lapping at the fluids draining from the corpses.

The twenty-second and twenty-third of November passed mostly without incident. Several more weapons caches were found, including a large one across the street from our eastern perimeter. A man had occupied the house across the street, claiming he was its owner. When Second Platoon had searched it, they'd found several dozen mortar rounds, half a dozen RPG rounds, and several machine guns. He later admitted he had been left as a security element to guard the weapons cache for a local Mujahedin group. He was taken into custody and sent to a local holding facility. Late in the afternoon of the twenty-third, the mortuary affairs team finally picked up the two bodies outside the western wire. The two dark stains that remained on the pavement served as stark reminders of their presence.

CHAPTER 16

We began a two-day patrol early in the morning of November 24 into an upscale residential neighborhood on the city's southwest side. We would be staying overnight in the area due to the many houses we had to search. The company hadn't seen any enemy contact since First Platoon's casualties of the nineteenth.

We set off to our search area after the morning resupply from the battalion. We were walking through the city streets when someone noticed a child's toes poking out from underneath one of a courtyard's heavy metal doors. Lt. Wilkens halted the platoon and cleared the home.

Inside was a young African woman in her early twenties with a small child around five years old. She spoke little Arabic, but through our interpreter, we could discern that she had traveled to Iraq with her husband so he could fight the Jihad. Her husband had been killed in the fighting. Now she was sheltering in this home with her young child. Finding foreigners fighting with the Mujahedin was not that uncommon, but seeing their families was. I felt terrible for her; I knew she would have difficulty raising her child in a foreign war zone. There was little we could do beyond giving her several MREs before continuing our movement.

We soon reached our targeted search area. This section of the city had somewhat nicer homes than we had previously seen. The woodwork inside was more opulent, and their furniture was of higher quality. Sgt. Hayden told us this was likely the neighborhood of Saddam's Ba'ath Party loyalists. I didn't know if he was right or not, but the homes' quality demonstrated these people were wealthy.

We also began to find evidence of prior military service in many of the homes. While searching one of the homes, I found an Iraqi Supreme Worthiness Medal, a Ba'athist award for service in the Gulf War. Many of the houses contained memorabilia from the occupants' military service. We also found a lot of weapons caches in the buildings.

The caches were often marked so that fighters could quickly identify them while moving through the buildings. A cinder block hanging over a wall meant that there was a cache nearby. Once we identified this, it became easier to locate the munitions. We found and destroyed several before the end of the first day. My platoon consolidated into one large two-story residence for the evening. Third Squad secured the first floor of our patrol base.

We were resupplied with food and water by the company headquarters section during the night. We also planned our clearing mission for the next day. We had finished our current sector and were about to move on to another area. The new area was located near our battalion's boundary with Third Marines. Adjacent battalions had seen heavy fighting in the region over the past several days.

The night passed without any enemy contact. In the morning, the squad leaders received a final brief from Lt. Wilkens. It was Thanksgiving Day, 2004. While we were waiting to move out, I sat with Marku and talked. We didn't have anything important to converse about, so I asked how his family was doing, and he asked about mine. Both of us wished we were home with our families for Thanksgiving instead of in Iraq.

It took us about an hour to move to our new search area. The sun was shining, and it was becoming a hot day. We began our leapfrog technique of using a single squad to clear a residence while the others cleared the adjacent ones. First Squad was on our right flank, Second in the middle, and Third cleared the left. The entire platoon was spread over roughly half a block —close enough to maintain radio contact and to hear if anyone got into a firefight. Our Icom radios worked only intermittently in the dense urban terrain, so the sound of gunfire was our primary means of knowing if a squad made enemy contact.

We had just finished clearing a house when we heard heavy automatic gunfire from Third Squad's sector. Lt. Wilkens was traveling with us; he tried to raise Cpl. Pennock, the squad leader, on the

Icom. The transmission was garbled, but we could tell they were in contact. We immediately began to race toward the sound of gunfire.

I grew nervous as the gunfire increased. I kept repeating the marching cadence "left, right, left" in my head. I just wanted to make sure that I kept my legs moving as the shooting rose from a distant din to a massive roar. I didn't quite know what was happening, but I could tell it was getting bad in Third Squad's area.

As we neared their position, a head rose above a roof wall nearby. It belonged to LCpl. Esquibel, the scout sniper attached to our platoon. He yelled and motioned for us to stop. We were just about to cross an alleyway, and he warned that the enemy had a machine gun positioned to rake that alleyway as we crossed. If he hadn't stopped us, we would have run right into their kill zone.

He shouted for us to go around the block and come in from the opposite direction. He told Lt. Wilkens that a Squad had been ambushed—they had casualties, and he was moving to help suppress the enemy positions so the survivors could withdraw. With that, his head disappeared below the roof wall again.

We reversed course and went around the block to come in from the opposite direction. First Squad had established a support-by-fire position in an adjacent building by the time we got there. Cpl. Pennock was in the street frantically trying to get help to rescue his stricken squad. We quickly cleared the buildings adjacent to the ambush site. In the house next door, we found a tunnel dug into the floor. We didn't know where it led, but its most likely terminus was in the enemy-occupied building at Third Squad's position.

Lt. Wilkens ordered Second Squad to leave someone to secure the tunnel. Cpl. Laforce looked at me and told me to kill anything that crawled out of the hole. They then moved up to attempt to rescue the stricken marines. I was left alone, guarding a dark hole in the floor of an empty house. I could hear the sounds of shouting and gunfire from the courtyard next door as GySgt. Parry led the platoon in an assault on the building.

He ordered an AAV to breach the courtyard wall, providing the squad with a means of entry out of the enemy kill zone. LCpl. Esquibel had attacked the enemy machine guns after warning Lt. Wilkens, giving the platoon enough breathing space to force entry into the courtyard. GySgt. Parry led a squad of marines into the breach to secure the perimeter and recover the wounded and killed marines.

Cpl. Marku and LCpl. Holmes were dead in the courtyard. Marku had been shot, and a thermal grenade on his chest rig had exploded. Holmes had been shot at point-blank range by the machine gun. LCpl. Hodges was wounded and playing dead alongside one of the engineers. Initially, we couldn't find Rodriguez. Later he was discovered wounded, hiding behind the home's propane tank.

After recovering our wounded and dead, the entire platoon pulled back while Lt. Wilkens called in an airstrike. The commander approved a five-hundred-pound bomb, which leveled the complex and the enemy fighters inside.

We were later able to piece together what had happened. Third Squad had made entry into the courtyard and stacked up on the front door to clear the house. The house was an L shape, with the door at the top of the Cpl. Pennock stepped outside to radio a report to Lt. Wilkens when the enemy had opened fire with a machine gun from the rooftop. The men in the courtyard had had no place to run. Hodges and Rodriguez reported having to play dead because the enemy would fire at anyone who moved.

Esquibel had killed the enemy fighter on the rooftop, enabling the platoon to mount an effective response. He would be the second Bravo Company marine to be awarded the Navy Cross for his actions during the battle. He would turn down the award, citing personal reasons.

Our decimated platoon returned to the school after the airstrike came in. We arrived just as our Thanksgiving meal arrived in marmite containers in the back of an AAV. None of us felt like eating, but we cycled through the chow line as ordered. Our hands and boots were still caked in the dust and blood from the fighting. GySgt. Parry helped serve the food to us. Nobody said anything as we sat down to eat.

I ate my Thanksgiving dinner on a cot next to Houck. His boots were covered in Marku's blood from when he'd pulled him onto the medevac track. I heard muffled noises coming from Houck. I looked up from my government-grade mashed potatoes and saw tears running down his dust-coated face.

"His fucking blood is all over my boots," was all he said as he wiped the tears from his face. Nothing else needed to be said. I returned to my mashed potatoes.

As we were finishing up, Sgt. Hayden came into the room. "There's another operation starting tomorrow. We're going to finish clearing these assholes out of this area."

CHAPTER 17

Operation Deer Drive began on November 26, 2004. The plan for the operation was a simple hammer-and-anvil technique. One-eighth of the marines would serve as the hammer, sweeping through the city's southern residential areas and forcing any remaining insurgents out of the houses and into the open. Fighters who chose to flee would be flushed out against the waiting armored units ringing the city. They would be the anvil. The insurgents who choose to stay and fight would be destroyed. The entire operation was scheduled to take two days.

Bravo Company had sustained many losses over the previous three weeks of fighting, so the marines we had left behind to guard our equipment on Camp Fallujah were brought out. Second Squad received LCpl. Fonda back. Maxey had twisted his ankle earlier in the fighting, so we were still down a man. Our squad had been lucky; we were the only squad in the company who hadn't sustained a casualty from combat. This operation was designed to neutralize any remaining fighters in our sector, so I began to think I would make it out of the battle alive.

The entire company took part in the operation. Our base in the school was turned over to a platoon from another company, allowing us to free up all our manpower. We were in position just before 0800, with all platoons clearing more or less in the same direction. We had cleared only about three buildings before First Squad found a large weapons cache.

Lt. Wilkens called in an EOD team to destroy the cache, holding up the entire platoon's movement. We had cleared a partially destroyed building before the cache's discovery, so the squad holed up there to wait for the order to move. Houck and I sat outside in the courtyard, soaking in the sunlight and guarding the entryway. It took almost an hour for the EOD team to arrive and rig the munitions for demolition.

We moved inside when the order came over the radio to take cover. EOD advised it would be a massive explosion, so everybody covered their ears and got away from the windows. The explosion itself shook the building to its very foundation, despite the 300 m distance between it and us. Once the dust had settled, Houck and I went back outside to resume our security position.

I had just sat down when he came over to me with a small bird gingerly cupped in his filthy hands. He opened his hands enough for me to see that the poor creature had been injured by debris from the blast. Blood was running from its side onto his fingers. It was terrified, throwing its head from side to side and trying to escape his grasp.

"I found him over there in the rocks," he said as

he nodded toward the entrance. "Must have been trying to fly away from the explosions."

I could tell he was in a moral dilemma. To spare the animal would mean that it would suffer needlessly, but I didn't think he wanted to see any more death. He looked at it for a few moments, clearly debating what to do. Thankfully, he didn't have to choose. After several minutes, the small bird passed; its maimed body grew limp in his hands. He laid it back down in the rocks where he had found it and brushed his bloody hands on his pants.

Sgt. Hayden walked outside, followed by the rest of the squad. It was time to move. We entered the next house and began our search. We found nothing in it. I climbed on top of the outdoor privy and looked underneath the water tank on top of the roof. We had often found weapons stashed underneath those water tanks.

As I was looking, I thought I heard a shuffling sound from the house next door. I froze and strained my ears to listen. Laforce looked up at me and asked if I had found something. I listened for another second and heard nothing. I looked down at him and said, "No, I don't think so."

We entered the next courtyard in a file. The building was an L-shape, just like the one where Third Squad had been ambushed. Neely and Fonda posted outside to pull security on the entrance. The rest of us began to clear the house.

The main door opened into the living room.

Laforce and I were the first into the room. He buttonhooked left, so I went across and posted at the far end of the room. The door at the far end was closed. Houck, Bowman, and Landers swept through the door behind us and stacked on the closed door. Hayden and Gravano brought up the rear, leaving Neely and Fonda outside.

Houck turned to Bowman and said, "Are you ready?" Bowman nodded, so Houck reached for the handle of the closed door. He had just begun to open it when the enemy fired the first round. A wall of dust and tracers rose from the wall surrounding the door, blocking out everything. The last thing I saw before the dust cloud engulfed him was Houck slamming the door shut again.

The insurgents had placed a machine gun on a table on the other side of the closed door. As Houck had begun to open the door, the enemy fighter had raked the room with 7.62 mm fire. Time seemed to slow down as the entire room became engulfed with darkness from the dust unleashed by the fiery bullets. The only light I could see through all the dust was the wall of tracers between me and the door and a window behind me.

I reached for the curtains on the window and threw them open, intending to jump out the window to escape the incoming fire. A burglar guard covered the window. I wouldn't be able to escape through there. I heard screaming and shouting; I thought everyone else had made it outside. I was trapped by the rounds racing through the air between me and escape.

I dove behind a love seat in the corner of the room. I thought to myself that this was the end of my life. I was convinced I was going to die. Despite this, I was oddly calm for a condemned man. If I was going to die, then I was going to die fighting. I took a good kneeling position behind the sofa and flipped my selector lever from safe to semi. I then began returning fire through the dust.

I dumped half a magazine into the doorway, but it didn't seem to reduce the amount of fire coming in through the walls. My 5.56 mm round didn't have the penetrating power of the enemy's 7.62 mm. I began to perceive that someone was next to me, behind an armchair. I peered through the thinning dust and saw Landers. His eyes locked onto mine, only two feet away. I looked at him as a tracer flew between us, causing us both to jump away from each other. I felt relieved that I wasn't alone.

After several minutes of frantic firing from both sides, the rate of fire began to slacken. As the dust cleared, I saw that the rest of my squad was in the room with me. They hadn't made it out as I'd initially thought. Hayden, Gravano, and Laforce were crouching behind a couch near the entranceway. Bowman was lying sprawled on the floor near the shot-up door. Houck was slumped on the floor by the still-closed door; his weight had kept the door closed despite the volume of fire passing through it. I believed he was playing dead, just as Rodriguez and Hodges had done the day before.

The door was riddled with holes. I could see enemy fighters running back and forth behind it. Gravano yelled out that he could see someone. I looked and could also see what appeared to be a man rushing at the door. We fired into him; the rounds seemed to keep him in the air for a second before he dropped. My rifle was on three-round burst, and I dumped another half-magazine into the figure. Our shooting caused the volume of enemy fire to increase for several minutes before it died down.

From everyone's frantic shouting, I discerned that the enemy had us trapped. Fighters on the rooftop had fired on Neely and Fonda, trapping them against the house. Another position in the kitchen had us pinned inside. We wouldn't be able to escape until we had neutralized the fighters on the roof, then killed the man in the kitchen. We had no communication with the rest of the platoon.

The fighter on the roof lobbed a grenade into the courtyard to try and kill Fonda and Neely. I heard it thud just outside of the barred window above my head seconds before it exploded. The force of the blast showered me with broken window glass. A piece about an inch long embedded itself into the bottom of my left palm. Fragments of glass covered my clothing and equipment. I heard Fonda yelling in the courtyard that the grenade had injured him.

I pulled the glass out of my hand and threw it on the ground. It was a deep cut, but it was superficial. I listened to Fonda scream for help in the courtyard. A piece of shrapnel had pierced his leg; he was having difficulty reaching his first aid kit. Nobody inside could help him, as we were all pinned down. After several minutes he crawled back into a position of relative cover against the wall of the house. The man on the roof would have to expose himself to reach him again.

I could hear GySgt. Parry shouting from the street outside. Sgt. Hayden relayed to him what was going on inside the house. Hayden yelled at Houck to ask if he was hurt. There was no response. Bowman crawled up next to him and grabbed his leg.

"I think Dave's had it," was all he could say.

That was the first time it occurred to me that Houck wasn't just pretending to be dead to avoid the fire. He had been killed in the initial salvo of fire. His final act had been to slam that door shut, masking the enemy fire and causing them to shoot blindly.

We continued to trade rounds with the insurgents for another hour or so. While this was happening, the rest of the platoon maneuvered into position outside the compound. At one point after a particularly intense exchange of gunfire, the enemy began shouting at us. We screamed obscenities back at them. This dialogue went on for several minutes before it devolved into the assholes chanting “Allahu Akbar” over and over again. We drowned out their whining with another burst of gunfire.

After about an hour, the rest of the platoon had surrounded the compound and brought up AAV support. When the tracks were set, GySgt. Parry screamed that he was coming in. Hayden warned him again about the enemy position in the kitchen, but Parry said he didn’t “give a fuck.” Parry grabbed Neely’s M249 SAW and rushed through the gated doorway into the enemy’s kill zone in the courtyard. Ignoring the danger, he rushed to the kitchen window and sprayed the enemy fighter inside with a burst of 5.56 mm link, screaming, “You die today, you fucking jihadi fucks!”

Around the same time, the sniper team killed the fighters on the rooftop. This created a window for us to extract ourselves from the building. Bowman grabbed Houck, and we pulled ourselves out. In my haste, I accidentally left behind the maul I’d been carrying. We beat a hasty retreat while Parry continued to dump a 200-round M249 SAW drum into the enemy position. He was the last one out of the courtyard after ensuring that all his marines had made it out.

We had spent over an hour trading rounds and insults with the insurgents in the house. I had entered that living room with fourteen magazines of thirty rounds; I left with four. We had received one marine WIA (Fonda) and one marine KIA

(Houck). We now had the insurgents surrounded and pinned down in the house. They still refused to surrender. We could hear their cries of "Allahu Akbar" over the gunfire and AAV engines.

I helped HN3 Markley, the company medic, load Houck's body onto a waiting AAV for evacuation to the rear. I helped lay him on the street as the ramp of the AAV began to drop. He lay on his back, his unblinking blue eyes staring blankly into the bright Iraqi sunlight. There was no spark in his eyes anymore. A bullet had pierced his cheek. It was a haunting scene. Earlier in the battle, he had asked me to send his necklace back home in the event of his death. I reached under his shirt to remove the chain, only to find it in pieces. The bullets that had slammed into his chest had destroyed the necklace. I quietly loaded him into the back of the waiting vehicle. My heart twisted as I realized he would never get to see his one-year-old daughter as he so desperately wanted.

Second Squad moved back to the building where Houck had found the injured bird to resupply our ammunition. We grabbed bandoleers of 5.56 mm and hand grenades from the other squads and quickly refilled our magazines. As we were doing this, Lt. Wilkens brought LCpl. Andres Llerena up with a S.M.A.W. rocket. He fired two missiles into the house to try and silence the enemy position. These two rockets were Llerena's 26th and 27th rockets during the battle. The blast destroyed the living room area we had just left but failed to silence the enemy fire completely.

After we had refilled our ammunition, Third Squad joined the rest of the platoon in suppressing the still-defiant insurgents. Lt. Wilkens ordered a D9 armored bulldozer to destroy the house. I watched as it rumbled up the road and into position. Its movement drew heavy fire from the insurgents still holed up in the house.

The armored dozer began to crush the building around the insurgents, yet the men inside refused to surrender. Their defiant chants of "Allahu Akbar" could still be heard over the continual din of automatic weapons fire. The bulletproof glass of the dozer was riddled with bullet holes, but the windows still held. Two insurgents tried to make a break for freedom, shooting from the hip as they ran out of the crumbling building. We shot them where they stood. At one point, the dozer's tracks ran over one of the dead insurgents as it was trying to reposition itself. His meat and flesh became entangled in the tracks, coating the vehicle's side in his gore.

The men inside fought to the very end, chanting about the greatness of God to the very end. Afterward, we cleared the rubble with fixed bayonets, looking for any survivors who may still be resisting. After combing through the ruins, we pulled out thirteen dead enemy fighters and one severely wounded. He was evacuated to the rear in an AAV. I never learned if he lived or died. We stacked the bodies in the street, one on top of the other like a bloody pile of wood. One of the dead men looked Asian. We speculated he was an Uyghur Muslim, but we had no way to prove it. Each of the fighters was carrying a zip lock bag with five hundred US dollars. The mortuary affairs detail would be by in the coming days to take them away. As we cleared the rubble, GySgt. Parry found my maul amid the destruction. He scolded me for being so careless with government property.

We'd spent the better part of the day dealing with this one pocket of enemy fighters. By the time we had finished clearing the rubble and evacuating the wounded and dead from both sides, it was almost dark. The platoon took an overwatch position in a nearby house. GySgt. Parry assigned a watch rotation for security before everyone bedded down.

My watch rotation was in the middle of the night. I sat on the rooftop overlooking the bloody pile of bodies. I could see the local stray dogs tearing chunks of flesh from the corpses under the starry sky. I felt nothing as I watched them fight over the scraps of our enemies.

The next day we continued our offensive. Third Platoon saw no real contact, but Second Platoon had their own trial by fire. They encountered another pocket of resistance, and it played out just like our two incidents. They gained entry into the house, only to be ambushed at close range. This technique enabled the enemy to negate our heavy armor and thermobaric weapons systems. One of

Second Platoon's engineer attachments, LCpl. Josh Lucero, was killed in the engagement.

First Platoon also lost a marine. Cpl. Kirk Bosselmann, one of the attached scout snipers, was killed on a rooftop. His death brought the total number of KIA for Bravo Company to thirteen marines over nineteen days.

Operation Deer Drive ended when Bravo Company reached the edge of the city. The last building we cleared was still under construction. We found nothing as we moved through the building; its brick framework marked the city's edge and the beginning of the desert. I looked out over the setting sun and saw the armored "anvil" that was waiting to catch the fleeing insurgents. I wondered if any insurgents had tried to flee or if they had all waited to die in close combat with us. We moved back to the school to rest and refit.

We spent the next few days patrolling the local area around the school. The company continued to find and destroy weapons caches, but we received no further contact. We could still hear sporadic gunfire throughout the city over the next several days, but we had effectively retaken Fallujah.

On the first of December, we abandoned the school we had been stationed in and moved into the city's industrial district. We occupied an old warehouse and began the process of refortifying it. Our daily patrols continued, but the enemy hadn't fortified the area. The number of weapons caches drastically decreased before drying up to a trickle. We could still hear the occasional gunfire off in the distance, but it was nothing like it had been in the weeks prior.

On December 7th, we were relieved in place by another battalion and rotated back to Camp Fallujah. We had spent a total of twenty-nine days in the city. We had several days to rest before resuming patrols on the outskirts of the city. Some of the brass had beer brought in as a thank-you for a job well done. Every marine in the battalion got two cans of beer. We started a bonfire on the base and sat around enjoying our first drinks since leaving the States. I wasn't technically old enough to drink, but they made an exception.

We finished up our tour conducting security patrols around the town of Al-Karmah, a rural suburb approximately sixteen kilometers from the city. The town had been a lifeline to the insurgents during the fight, funneling weapons and supplies into the city. The area immediately outside the town served as the graveyard for the fighters killed in the battle. We would pass rows of fresh graves during our patrols.

We didn't see much fighting during our month in Al-Karmah. Most of the surviving fighters had gone to ground in the aftermath of the conflict, and it would be several months before they resurfaced. Bravo Company's brief tenure in the area was relatively calm. Our most significant concerns were the occasional rocket or mortar fired at Camp Fallujah and avoiding falling into one of the canals that ran through the area. Third Platoon received no further contact after we rotated out of the city.

The battalion began to rotate back to Al Asad Airbase in late January 2005. Most of Third Platoon left Camp Fallujah in the back of trucks on a cold, dark January night. I was fortunate that I was selected to fly in a helicopter due to my "promotion" into the company headquarters section. My next assignment was as the company arms room custodian; the previous incumbent was Sgt. Hudson. He had been shot on the 9th of November.

I watched what was left of my platoon load into the trucks for the journey. I thought of our trip out of ASP Wolf two months prior. There were a lot fewer of us now. I helped close the tailgate on the trucks and stood on the side of the road, watching them drive away into the darkness.

I flew back to Al Asad on January 25, riding a CH-53E Super Stallion out of Camp Fallujah. We flew back to the States on January 30. The battalion hosted a family reception in the on-post gym, but a six-hour delay caused our return to occur in the middle of the night. This delay drastically muted the expected fanfare. The buses dropped us off in front of the battalion armory in the dead of night. We silently queued up to turn in our weapons before drifting off. Some men met their wives at the gym, but most of us went off to the barracks. Doc Lambotte greeted me at the barracks with a bottle of whiskey.

After getting shot on the first day of the battle, he had been sent to the Bethesda Naval Hospital in Bethesda, Maryland. He took leave from the hospital to see our return. I proceeded to get blackout drunk for three days.

AFTERWARD

It was a gloomy, overcast morning on Camp Lejeune. It had rained the night before, but the sun was slowly starting to peer out through the clouds. I glared up at the clouds, thinking that if only the sun could burn off the overcast clouds, it would be a beautiful spring day.

I put on my best uniform and made my way outside for formation. The entire battalion was making its way towards the base gym for a memorial service. We were saying goodbye to the Marines we had lost during the deployment. We had been back for almost two months, long enough to go home on leave and begin to regain some semblance of normal.

We formed by platoons in the parking lot of the battalion. The gray sky cast long shadows on everyone's faces. Family members dotted the ground as they made their way individually towards the base gym. We marched in silence down the street towards the gym.

I watched the long lines of men begin to march towards the gym, and I could not help but think of the odd coincidences of war. I wondered whether it was a random chance that some men were spared while others were not, or was there a divine hand in it. Random chance had determined who was shot and who was not. I felt that skill mattered less than luck; how else could I justify surviving while so many others had not.

The ceremony itself was brief yet poignant. The families of the fallen men were present. The ceremony was the first time I met many of them. In my mind, I had always seen these men as Marines, fighting in Iraq just as I was. Seeing their mother, fathers, brothers, and sisters added a human dimension to them that I had not anticipated. It was challenging to speak with them. I found myself trying to justify in my mind why I had survived and their loved ones had not.

The finality of death was on full display in the center of the gymnasium floor. An inverted rifle, a bayonet, a set of dog tags, and a pair of boots represented each fallen man. Thirteen of these memorials represented men from Bravo Company. Chaplain Cox led those assembled in prayer before the commander read a speech. The battalion watched the solemn ceremony from the bleachers. The families of the fallen sat alone at tables on the gym floor.

The battalion memorial service was one of the last times the entire platoon assembled in the same place. Many people either got out or changed duty positions immediately afterward. The wounded who could travel all made the long trip from the military hospitals to Camp Lejeune for the service. It was good to see Lambotte, Rodriguez, Crist, and the others.

Afterward, I went to lunch with Houck's parents and most of Third Squad. His family asked questions about how he had died. I could tell they were curious but trying not to upset any of us by digging too deep. We answered their questions as best as we could. Meeting everyone's families left me with a deeper appreciation of the human costs of military operations.

Within three months of redeployment, the platoon looked completely different due to the high turnover in personnel. Most of the senior guys were at the end of their service contracts. They mostly left the Marines and rejoined the civilian world. Those that remained quickly found themselves in another training cycle as the battalion prepared for yet another deployment. The battalion was awarded the Navy Unit Commendation for the deployment.

The conflict in Iraq continued for years after the Second Battle of Fallujah. I never concerned myself with the ebbs and flows of US involvement in Iraq. My only focus was finishing my enlistment, going to college, and living the rest of my life. I spent four years in the Marine Corps before being discharged on June 22, 2007. I slowly lost touch with most members of the platoon over the years.

When I think about my time in Iraq, I am reminded of how lucky I really was. I walked away from the incident relatively unscathed; many of my comrades in arms did not. The cost of war is evident in the scars they bear on their minds and bodies. Many suffer from the long-term effects of PTSD, physical disabilities, and broken relationships.

GLOSSARY OF TERMS

AAV: Assault Amphibious Vehicle, the AAVP-7A1

ACOG: Advanced Combat Optical Gunsight made by Trijicon

AK-47: A Russian 7.62mm rifle commonly used throughout the world

AT-4: An 84mm single-use anti-tank rocket used by US forces

ASP: Ammunition Supply Point, where munitions are stored

BFT: Blue Force Tracker, a computer program that identifies the location of friendly units

CQ: Charge of Quarters, the noncommissioned officer in charge of the barracks

D9: An armored bulldozer

EOD: Explosive Ordnance Disposal, the engineer squad responsible for unexploded devices

FiST: Forward Infantry Support Team, the name for the artillery observers attached to the company

FOB: Forward Operating Base

HLZ: Helicopter Landing Zone

HMMWV: High Mobility Multipurpose Wheeled Vehicle, a term for the Humvee family of vehicles

IED: Improvised Explosive Device

KIA: Killed in Action

M240: A US-made 7.62mm medium machinegun

MARPAT: Marine Pattern, the name for the Marine Corps camouflage pattern

MCLC: Mine Clearing Line Charge, used to create a breach in minefields

MEU: Marine Expeditionary Unit

MOUT: Military Operations in Urban Terrain

MRE: Meals Ready to Eat, prepackaged rations

NCO: Noncommissioned Officer

NVG: Night Vision Goggles

OPFOR: Opposing Force

PAS-13: A thermal optic sight used to see heat signatures

PKM: A 7.62mm belt-fed medium machine gun originally produced in the Soviet Union

POG: People Other than Grunts, a derogatory term used by the infantry to describe non-infantry people

POO: Point of Origin, describes where a mortar or artillery round originated from

PX: Post Exchange, the name of military run stores

PT: Physical Training

RCT: Regimental Combat Team

RTO: Radio Telephone Operator

RPG: Rocket Propelled Grenade

RPK: A Soviet 7.62mm light machine gun

SAW: M249 Squad Automatic Weapon, a 5.56mm belt-fed light machinegun

S.M.A.W.: Mk 153 Shoulder-Launched Multi-purpose Assault Weapon is a shoulder-launched rocket used against tanks

SOI: School of Infantry

WIA: Wounded in Action

RANKS OF THE UNITED STATES MARINE CORPS

Enlisted

PVT: Private
PFC: Private First Class
LCpl: Lance Corporal
Cpl: Corporal
Sgt: Sergeant
SSgt: Staff Sergeant
GySgt: Gunnery Sergeant
1st Sgt: First Sergeant
SgtMaj: Sergeant Major

Officer

2nd Lt: Second Lieutenant
1st Lt: First Lieutenant
Capt: Captain
Maj: Major
LtCol: Lieutenant Colonel
Col: Colonel

Made in the USA
Monee, IL
02 May 2021

67485101R00114